The Divorced Mom's Guide to Dating

How to Be Loved, Adored, and Cherished

Mai Vu

Download The Worksheets – Free

Just to say thank you for purchasing my book, I would like to offer you a set of printable worksheets to accompany this book. You can download them here: http://maivucoach.com/book-worksheets/

Published by Simply Good Press, Montclair, NJ / A division of Jane Tabachnick and Co.

ISBN: 978-0692664469

This publication is designed to provide accurate and authoritative information with regard to the subject matter covered. It is sold with the understanding the publisher is not engaged in rendering relationship, legal or other professional advices. If professional assistance is required, the services of a competent professional should be sought. The opinions expressed by the author in this book are not endorsed by Simply Good Press, and are the sole responsibility of the author rendering an opinion.

For information contact: Simply Good Press at 646 867-0788 or visit us online at: http://www.simplygoodpress.com

DEDICATION

This book is dedicated to all the hard-working moms around the world, who put everyone else's needs first, starving themselves of love and support, yet expecting to raise healthy children, have a successful business or career, and still have time and energy to maintain a decent relationship with a man. I want to show you a new way to accomplish everything you want to achieve while being loved, adored, and cherished by everyone around you, especially your man!

ACKNOWLEDGMENTS

This book would not have been possible without the support and encouragement of so many people. First, I would like to thank the big Universe for channeling the 3Ps™ concept to me. This gift has helped me and my clients make sense out of our crazies and allowed us to create an amazing Hot Life with Hot Love and a Hot Business too. Second, I would like to thank my parents for being so courageous to escape out of Vietnam so that I could have all the opportunities in the palms of my hands. I especially would like to thank my mother for her innate wisdom of how a woman should be loved and cared for, and how she should treat herself with dignity, love, and respect. I would like to thank my brother, Sonni Vu, for his gentle and generous support in the last twenty years, as he watched me build my business while learning what the Universe had to teach me. It was a scary process for my family. Sonni was always there with "What do you need, Sis?"

Next I would like to thank all of my clients who believed in my work, took it to heart, and came back to affirm to me that this concept works. Not only that, some have stepped up to champion me and brought me into their circle of friends and families. Cindy Ashton, thank you for helping me give birth to the 3Ps™ concept. Maria Appelqvist, thank you for bringing me to Sweden and showing me that my concept is universal, not just for American women. Linda Lyngso for your generous love and support over the years. Anna Åberg for the full embodiment of the 3Ps™. To these clients and so many more: Jessica Olofsson, Anna Bergström, Annika Isacsson, Anja Callius (who brought me to Stockholm), Veronica Sundström, Jeanette Niemi, Cindy Roemer, Jo Ellen Neihart, Anne Kirwan, Mina Truong, Kira Edwards, Petra Carlsson, Viktoria Davidsson, Kiriaki Christoforidis, Astrid Seter, Åsakarin Gunnarsson, Raluca Hariz, Git Guldare, Annelie Ivarsson, Ewa Äckerlind, Pamela Butterweck, Bindu Ann Joseph, Eva Sjöstedt, Miryam Bäckström, Lenora Cooper, Darla Crecerelle, Anita Carlsson, Britta Sjöström, Suzanne Aziz, Karen Sabaten, Andrea Williams, Denise Barragan, Ara Lucia, Connie Payne, Elaine Wegenka. THANK YOU! I love, adore, and cherish you.

I was blessed with several super heroines who helped me serve my clients. Without them, no one would have heard of me: Nicole Huguenin, Lynne Sagen, Leslie Rivera, Michelle Metz, Jane Tabachnick. To my teachers, I am deeply grateful: The Coaches Training Institute Leadership team, Flo Hoylman, Nicole Daedone, Mark and Shannon, Home Nguyen. To my besties: Shariann Tom and Kelly Wolf, thank you for our forever friendship.

Finally, thank you to my lovely, yummy girl, Maia Vu-Minnich, who teaches me how to be a Princess, and to my hot man, Keith Cuddeback, who shows me what being loved, adored, and cherished looks and feels like. I am forever grateful.

PREFACE: A LOVE NOTE FROM MAI VU

Dear Divorced, Single and Married Moms (too),

I know what it's like to be single and dating again. It sucks! I've been there and done that. Whatever happened to our fairy tale marriage, right? Shouldn't we live happily ever after? What about the kids? Who would want us? Besides, who has time to date? We are exhausted with doing everything and being there for everyone else. Frankly, "Ain't nobody got time for that!"

Well, congratulations for picking up this book. I know there are lots of dating books out there. But I promise you this one is unlike all the other books. Once you understand my 3Ps™ concept, you will not have to work so hard at anything in life again, let alone dating. You will learn how to shift so that you will be loved and supported in all your endeavors. Then, because of your newfound way of being, you will naturally attract that hot man, your greatest love affair into your life. You will see that relationship, dating, and even success are easy and right in front of you. It's not elusive and frustrating like it has been.

Thank you for everything you do in your life to make a difference. It's now your turn to be loved, adored, and cherished so that you are joyously creating a new life with your ideal companion by your side, loving you every step of the way. Let's get you ready for your HotLifeHotLove™.

Love, Love, Love,

Mai Vu

ABOUT THE COVER PHOTO

Ten years ago when my marriage fell apart, I grabbed my four-year-old daughter and ran away to Cannon Beach in Oregon for a week. I could not afford much. Somehow I got a reservation at this dumpy motel that has a yearlong wait list, which was the least expensive option, yet was located right on the beach. While there, I tended to my daughter and wondered what would happen to us. Would I ever find love again?

Nine years later, my sweetheart of seven years surprised me with a road trip for my forty-ninth birthday to the Oregon coast. Guess where we stayed? In the fancy hotel that was three doors down from the old, dumpy hotel on Cannon Beach. All my wishes came true... I am with a wonderful man who loves, adores, and cherishes me. My daughter is healthy, beautiful, and thriving. My business is rocking it and I am having a worldwide impact.

This picture is a reminder that dreams do come true. I had to learn to trust again, to let love in, and to learn to be loved, adored, and cherished. It's easier said than done.

Photo Credit: Keith Cuddeback, **Essence In Photography**
http://www.essenceinphotography.com/

CONTENTS

- Origin of the book
- How to Use this Book

- Meet Peasant Mai
- Worksheet #1: How Did You Develop Your Peasant Traits?
- How Does the Peasant Date?
- Worksheet #2: Are You Dating Like a Peasant?
- The Results of Peasant Dating
- Worksheet #3: Listen to Your Peasant pain
- What is Your Peasant Role?

- Worksheet #4: Discovering Your Princess
- How Do You Know Your Princess Self?
- Listening to Your Princess

FOREWORD

There are few things more mystical in nature than love—and not just romantic love, but all types of love, from sisterhood to caretaking to self-love. Mai Vu, and her work with what she calls the 3Ps™, demystifies romantic love by providing practical guidance for cultivating love in our everyday lives, particularly in the area of dating. Through radical honesty and a desire for every woman (and man) to have the love of their life, Mai is an agent of transformation.

I know this because she played a large part in transforming my life. I worked for Mai as her business manager for two years while also participating in her program. Some would say this might create a bias; however, this also meant that I had twenty-four-hour access to her, her work, and her clients. For two years I was on the front lines with hundreds of women from around the world who were sick and tired of being sick and tired. In as little as six months, I witnessed many women transform their relationships and their lives. From first dates to new romances to second marriages to blending families to jet-setting and building careers, I watched as women stopped waiting for love to find them, stopped waiting at home for their man to pay attention to them, and instead reclaimed themselves as the love-filled, beautiful women they always were.

For me personally, I had come to a juncture where the status quo wasn't going to work anymore. I knew well what I *didn't* want in love and work, but I had no clue what I truly desired for my life, let alone how to go about getting it. After dating a slew of depressed, emotionally unavailable men, and feeling totally exhausted at my job as a high school teacher, I habitually put myself and my needs last, always ending up in same lackluster relationships and resentment-filled work. Then I met Mai.

As I embarked on the journey of creating a great life over a good-enough one, Mai helped me every step of the way. She's no pom-pom cheerleader; she is right there in the game playing with you, holding your hand while you heal from resentments (that hard-working, people pleaser inside all of us), encourage your inner beauty to come out and play (trust me, as a lifelong tomboy I fought this concept as if I were fighting off a dragon), and learn to know, trust, and stand in your deepest knowings and power.

Without this work, I never would have had the confidence to start my own business and become a co-owner of a second. Working with Mai gave me the courage, energy, and knowledge to be what I call a generosity entrepreneur. After a chance encounter with a seventy-two-year-old woman in 2012, I founded Wild Dream Walks, an organization that brings one's wildest dreams to fruition as a community. In 2015, I committed to walking each day with a new person as a means of valuing connection over transaction. After walking with thousands of people, I feel I now lead my life with love as the truest bottom line.

In terms of dating, every man I've seriously dated in the past few years is closer and closer to what I want. (Let's face it, the fact that I even know what I want and can have that in a relationship, dating or otherwise, is reason enough to read this book!) My relationships with men have changed drastically. Every day I am thankful for the tools Mai taught me to relinquish any and all bitterness, hurt, and hopelessness. The drama that comes from longing and neediness has been replaced with wonderful heart connections, soul meetings, and even meaningful good-byes. I am no longer attached to making any relationship work. Rather, I'm committed to falling madly in love with myself and trusting that the person who falls in love with me will love, adore, and cherish every part of who I am. That man, I know, will come sooner rather than later.

There's no doubt in my mind that reading this book will open your heart again and teach you how to keep it open. That's really what my work with Mai accomplished. She truly wants us all to lead hot lives and have hot loves, and she won't settle for anything less. Although she might present you with some truths that are hard to swallow, I can promise you that her methods work. Over the years, I've watched client after client find her man and, more importantly, find her own happiness. Although this book is written as a practical guide for divorced women who are dating again, its contents can be applied to any woman who desires deep love in her life. I urge you to show up to Mai's words and her guidance. If you do this, your life will forever be changed (for the hotter, as she would say).

—Nicole Huguenin, Chief Dream Architect

* * *

When I first heard of Mai Vu's 3Ps™, I didn't see myself as a *peasant*. At that point, I had been a stage and presence coach, a professional speaker, and a singer and entertainer. I was offended by the thought that I was a mere "peasant," and I resented being identified or labeled as such. In my mind, I thought, *I am smart and educated, and I have done great things and made a name for myself. I am not a peasant!* But deep down I realized that I would not be that defensive unless there was something to what Mai was trying to teach me. So I took it on and reflected on it some more.

I realized that in our desire to step up and be powerful women, most of us have become slaves—or, to use Mai's term, "*peasants*." With something to prove, we work hard and push without realizing how that is leaving us depleted. As I dove in and saw how Mai's ideas showed up in my own life, I was shocked by how I was rendered into a powerless woman despite my accomplishments.

The biggest thing was that I was not clear on my boundaries and how I should be treated. I was not clear on what is acceptable, and a lot of times I oscillated between extremes, either bulldozing others by over asserting myself or playing the victim and staying silent when I knew I had something that should be heard. I didn't know how to ask for help without apology or shame. I constantly had to prove myself. Being an "empowered" woman left me exhausted, resentful, and tired, and I constantly felt like I had not done enough. Mai's insights helped me face the reality that while I had a great résumé, I was a slave to everyone and to myself. This stopped me from having the love and success that I truly wanted. I wasn't taking care of me. I kept saying yes when I couldn't or shouldn't. And I ended up creating chaos and dissatisfaction in my life.

Mai once invited me to be her houseguest. When I arrived, I was struggling to schlepp my luggage up a flight of stairs. Mai came down to help me and told me that I no longer had to carry my own luggage. I didn't need to try to prove that I was a strong and competent woman. I didn't need to prove anything. I saw then that I wasn't used to letting others help me. I was trying to do it all on my own because before that I didn't know any other way.

It was Mai who got me where I am today—truly nurtured, pampered, and feeling deeply at peace and in flow with my life. Since knowing Mai, I've received awards from President Obama and the Queen of England acknowledging my commitment to volunteerism, and I've appeared in multiple media outlets, including *The New York Times*, the *Metro News*, and *Performance Magazine*. I am honored and excited to recommend Mai's book to you because she will show you how to be and feel and *own* all of you. You get to have your voice and be heard.

In my experience, a lot of coaching and self-help books try to sell people an unrealistic and unattainable outcome. And when we fail to reach it, we feel even more shame, guilt, and disappointment for not having reached our goal—especially since we "did the work." With Mai, it's about getting real with yourself, and experiencing real and lasting change. There's no Pollyanna outlook, no false optimism that doesn't translate to the real work; just real, realistic guidance that will help you navigate the world and your life, dating and otherwise. Mai is not going to sell you an unachievable pipe dream; she helps you come to peace with yourself, step into your authentic power, ask for what you want, and get it from a grounded, strategic place.

Mai has helped make me who I am today, and I am overjoyed that she has finally gathered all of her wisdom into this book you are now holding. She is the first coach to set the standard of being the best life coach to me, and I know you will enjoy and benefit from the 3Ps™ as much as I have.

—Cindy Ashton, Award-Winning Singer and Speaker Coach

INTRODUCTION

The Origin of This Book

When I think of what it took for me to learn to love, to work, and to build successful relationships in my life, I credit two life-changing events. The first is my decision to leave the corporate world twenty years ago and become a life coach. The second is my decision to host a sex party with my husband when I turned thirty-nine.

When I left the corporate world in 1996, at the age of thirty-one, I wanted to find fulfillment. Up to that point, working and climbing the corporate ladder as an engineer helped satisfy my basic needs: safety and security, a monthly direct deposit, and a health care plan. It afforded me the opportunity to buy a house, get married, and give birth to my daughter. But I was not fully satisfied. Something was missing, and while I didn't know it then, I was being directed from within to reach for more satisfaction and fulfillment.

One week before I left my job, I received a fax from a girlfriend. It was a brochure on life coaching, and she'd scribbled next to it, "I think this is for you." Sight unseen, without any research, I signed up for the first course. My life completely changed from that weekend on, and I knew that I was now on the right path. For the next decade, I dedicated my life to becoming the best coach in the world. I trained with the best organization, The Coaches Training Institute. I became one of their senior trainers, and I traveled the world helping them develop life coaches for thirteen years.

I learned how to live life from a place of abundance, where I was encouraged to change the world with my passion instead of hard work; I learned to manifest and create instead of earning and proving myself; and I learned to trust and ask for help instead of protecting and fighting for personal causes.

Don't get me wrong, there is always a place for my old self, with her basic needs, to exist and do work in the world. I still work hard. Building a business is hard work, and I still cook, clean, parent my daughter, though she's more grown up now, etc. I still do all the necessary work that needs to be done, but now I approach it with a new outlook that makes life easier and more fun. I'll share a lot more with you about this new outlook throughout the book. For now, suffice it to say that it has to do with my discovery of what I call the 3Ps™: the Peasant, the Princess, and the Priestess.

When I was getting ready to turn thirty-nine, I truly hoped that I could coast for the rest of my life and somehow things would just magically get better. I watched my daughter grow up, and my then-husband and I grow older, and I didn't want any waves, any big changes. I had reached a place of certainty and security that had its own joy, satisfaction, and comfort. I didn't need any more growth and challenges—or so I thought.

One night, a few days before my birthday, I was getting a massage from my massage therapist, Michelle. With my face down, she asked me, "So, what are you going to do for your birthday?" I was empty for a moment, then I heard a voice from deep inside of me say, *Put on a sex party.*

My body jolted so hard, I almost fell off the table. The thoughts came flooding in. *What?! I don't know what that is! Why would I want to do that? I can't do that! I am a mom, a businesswoman, a teacher, a wife. I can't do that!* But the voice replied, simple and succinct: *Are you going to let us out, or are you going to kill us off in this lifetime?*

That voice inside, what we call our intuition, knows exactly what is needed. Did I dare listen to her? That voice is not always rational, appropriate, or practical. I asked myself again: *Do I dare listen to her?*

I immediately broke into tears on the table because I knew she was right. As much as I had developed my mind and my heart to learn and grow, I was petrified of my sexuality. And I had been on a secret mission to lock it up for the rest of my life.

I did decide to have the sex party for my thirty-ninth birthday, and I never regretted it. What happened next deserves a book by itself, but I'll try to summarize it briefly for you here:

With my husband's support, I had my sex party, which opened up a whole new world. It was there that I learned about unconditional love for the first time and started my journey to reclaim my relationship to my sex and sexuality. After that night, my husband and I opened up our marriage to include new partners. It was an amazing and courageous journey that we were totally unprepared for, which created both disastrous and life-changing outcomes.

Then my marriage broke apart. My husband moved out, went into a deep hole, and was forced to face all the things he had been avoiding in himself, trying to love me and my daughter. After he left, I went on a three-year journey (what I call my personal PhD program) to learn about my sex. I wanted to separate sex, love, and relationship so that I could understand how I love, how I am in relationship, and who I am as a sexual being. The insights I gained by separating these three things that are so easily entwined were profound, and I'll share more about them in a later chapter.

I went from having been with just one man, my then-husband, to experiencing thirty-three men in three years. I reclaimed my power and my sexuality. I taught myself how to date and took back my power and rightful place as a hot, beautiful, smart woman. I broke all of my previous codependency patterns surrounding dating and men. I realized that when it came to love and dating, even though I was thirty-nine years old, I was repeating terrible relationship behaviors that I'd learned during my teenage years. Finally, I healed my relationship and wounds with men. I was no longer afraid, distrusting, or dependent on them.

Today, I am thrilled to be with a partner who loves, adores, and cherishes me. My ex-husband knew how to love me. But he didn't know how to adore and cherish me. Furthermore, I didn't know how to cultivate that in our relationship. My current partner, Keith, loves this concept of the 3Ps™. And we practice it with each other daily—though I've had to adapt it a little bit to suit him. Instead of having a Peasant, Princess, and Priestess, he has a Peasant, a King, and a Magician. It doesn't have the same ring to it as the woman's 3Ps™, but it still works. I help him love his *peasant* self, step into his rightful *king* place, and develop his access to his *magician* self. In return, he takes great care of my *peasant* so that I can soften up and surrender to my *princess* self, which allows me to be so much more joyful, fun, and at ease. Beyond that, he helps me behind the scenes with getting my message out into the world because he is inspired and called forth by my *priestess*. He gets how important it is for the world to hear me, and he gladly feels a sense of honor to serve and protect me (his words). This is what being cherished looks like.

I have built my business from a pure *peasant* place (I can do it myself). And I am now building it from my integrated 3Ps™, where I am loved, adored, and cherished by my man and all people who are in relationship with me. I can tell you, it's a lot more fun, powerful, successful, and easy to build from a place of the 3Ps™. Furthermore, I truly think that we are all called to make a difference in the world, and for that to happen it is essential for us to do our work from a place of being loved, adored, and cherished. This is how we will sustain ourselves, have the greatest impact, and do it from an authentic and powerful place.

I hope that after reading this book you will see that what you are up to is a lot bigger and a lot more important than just dating. As you learn to undo your *peasant* mindset and step into your *princess* and *priestess* selves, you will naturally attract the man who will resonate with what you want. He will appreciate your hard-working self, bring out your softer side, and champion you toward your cause. He will treat you with love, adoration, and respect, and you will do the same for him.

How to Use This Book

This book is in a question-and-answer format, and reflects my responses to questions from the media, clients in seminars, and private counseling sessions collected over a twenty year period. Some of the questions and answers are what I said verbatim, while others represent what I've said generally to people who share similar problems. I hope that this format is helpful and allows you to clearly and quickly find the answers to some of your own questions.

In the course of 8 chapters, we'll cover who your Peasant, Princess, and Priestess are, as well as the roles they play in your dating life and your everyday life as a whole. We'll identify and clear the resistance that your *peasant* has the tendency to put on you, we'll practice being a *princess*, and we'll learn how to empower and cultivate your *priestess* so that you can do your work in the world. We'll look at the distinction between love, sex, and relationships, and, of course, we'll talk a whole lot about dating as a divorced working mother. My approach may be unconventional, but I promise I've helped hundreds of women identify their 3Ps™ and go on to find loving, healthy relationships.

Note: This book is not meant to replace the help of a professional therapist, psychologist, or coach, who can offer specific guidance, in person, that is tailored to you and your progress. I offer these services myself, and I would never set a client loose with this book and say it's all they need for success. Guidance, regular feedback, encouragement, and course correction from a professional cannot be replaced. However, this book is an excellent place to begin in terms of helping bring you back in touch with yourself.

I encourage you to practice the exercises throughout the chapters, as they will help you begin to remember and reclaim who you are. Just reading about these concepts is not enough—you also need to apply them and practice referring to them in everyday situations. Once internalized, I think you'll find it's second nature to identify which part of yourself is shining though at any moment—Peasant, Princess, or Priestess. And you honestly need all three to thrive in dating and in life. I want you to have a hot life and hot love. Let's get started!

CHAPTER ONE

The Peasant

Let's begin with the Peasant, shall we?

Yes, that's the ideal place to begin. The *peasant* is me and she is you. It's the physical part of you who lives on this planet, wakes up in the morning, has twenty-four hours in a day, has all the duties and responsibilities of being a daughter, a sister, a best friend, a wife, a mom, and so on.

The *peasant* just wants to be good, to do things right. I hear my clients say things like, "I just want to be the best I can be for the people around me." "I strive for excellence in everything I do." "I want to be perfect. If it is not perfect, I don't want to do it." You hope that if you are good enough, and if you do enough, then you will feel like you are worthy enough for love. Often you are run by a deep sense of guilt and fear that you are not enough and have not done enough. All you ask for is to be loved, to have a roof over your head, and to have money and security so that you can retire and live a happy and peaceful life with a nice partner.

So often you are so entrenched in your *peasant* that you lack community and support. You don't trust anyone. Your complaints are that no one understands you, people gossip about you, and that you are treated unfairly. You rush around to do things for others, for your work, for your children. Yet deep down inside you've lost your sense of purpose. You are responsible for everyone except yourself. You let yourself get overweight or out of shape. Then you believe that no one will love you because you are ugly and unattractive. You lost your dreams somewhere along the way. You continue to deplete yourself and you become more and more resentful because you are forgotten. You are harsh on yourself, impatient, and disgusted with how you feel.

You do not value or honor your time and energy. You give both away freely and indiscriminately. Then you complain that you are exhausted and too overwhelmed to date or take care of yourself. You are afraid to say no because you might upset someone. You make excuses for people's bad behavior and disrespect toward you.

Last, you want so much to be chosen, pursued, and loved by a man, yet you feel unworthy and undeserving. If you don't chose, pursue, or love yourself, how can you let anyone else do it for you? He could be standing right in front of you all along, and you don't even see him.

Does a Peasant need to be cultivated, or does she naturally exist?

Life cultivates the *peasant.* I believe that we are all born *princes* and *princesses.* When I was born, I know my mom loved me. She thought my brother and I were precious, and she devoted herself to us. The day we came out of her belly, at least for that one day, we (most of us human beings) were *princes* and *princesses.* Our mother looked at us and said, "I promise to take care of you and love you forever." But over time our parents might not have been as available, or worst case, some parents have to give their kids away, but still there is a part of us that can remember feeling like we were born as *princes* and *princesses.*

Then life teaches us to become *peasants.* It could happen on day one, or in the first year, or the third year, or whenever. One day, we look up at Mom and Dad and realize, *Oh my gosh, life is really scary. I've got to protect myself. I've got to take care of myself. I've got to earn all my love, or else these people might abandon me. I'm just a lump. But look, if I smile, they smile back. That feels good. I'm going to keep smiling...This is how I earn love.*

Earning love begins really early. And then we see Dad angry, and Mom not able to cope with her life, and we start to develop opinions and beliefs about life, which form the basis of our *peasant*: put your head down, work hard, limit yourself, and keep out of trouble. These are coping mechanisms.

Even if we are spoiled, we can still be *peasants*.

When we don't get enough love and attention, we develop this overarching *peasant* figure. Remember, though, that it's not about recognizing and eliminating the *peasant* in favor of pursuing the *princess* and *priestess*. That is not my message. We need all three parts to thrive. You need the *peasant* because she works in this real world. With her *princess* and *priestess*, your *peasant* feels stronger, safer. She knows your birthright, and what she is truly capable of. When you're just one part without the other two, things are imbalanced.

Meet Peasant Mai

Before we dive any deeper, I want to share a bit more about where I came from and why I am qualified to teach you how to date again.

I am a total *peasant* when it comes to my past. I was born in the middle of the Vietnam War to a struggling middle-class family. My mom was a very famous television anchorwoman in the sixties on one of the only TV stations in Vietnam. My dad had nothing.

I watched my parents struggle and fight for the first eighteen years of my life. I saw how difficult it was for my mom to juggle being a well-known celebrity and being married to a man who was "lesser" than she was. I also felt my dad's pain of trying to love and please my mom. And no matter how much they tried, they didn't seem to see eye to eye on anything. Every night as a child, I wished and prayed that they would divorce.

Watching their marriage unfold and listening to my mother's logic about men and relationships instilled *peasant* beliefs in me, like "A good man is hard to find," and "A man can't be successful/powerful and loving and loyal at the same time." When I grew up, I would have to pick one or the other. My mother chose a loving and loyal man. And she lived out the consequences of being with someone who didn't have the same drive and capacity to achieve greater power and success.

Peasant Trait #1: I learned to compromise and choose less in a man.

My dad was a poor soldier who didn't measure up by society's standards. He was very angry and scared about his life. His dad had died when he was four years old and his mom was extremely harsh. My dad grew up unstable and volatile. He loved us dearly, but his form of parenting was to hit my brother and me into submission. I can't tell you how many beatings I had as a child for nothing. If I did a math problem incorrectly, broke a dish, or spilled a Coke at a restaurant I was slapped hard across my face. The marks of his rage and disappointment toward his life ended up on my brother and my bodies most of the time.

Peasant Trait #2: Big men are scary; always duck and cover. Don't stand up to a man; he will hit me down.

Peasant Trait #3: Love is confusing and scary. It's good one minute, and it can be super scary and volatile the next. So always be on guard; if I relax I will be hurt.

I grew up to be really good, *really* responsible. I took care of my little brother and went to a Catholic girls' school. I was a terrible student, and was not in the right place with the right support. I remember walking to school at seven years old, wondering about my life and thinking, *Why am I here? Why am I in the wrong place? Why is it so hard?*

I tried hard at school, but I kept failing and failing. My parents were called into the principal's office more times than I care to remember. They were so ashamed and frustrated with me. I tried to make up for my trouble in school by being really responsible around the house.

Peasant Trait #4: I learned to blame myself. If only I was good enough.

Peasant Trait #5: I must try harder, take on other responsibilities to prove to people around me that I am good enough and that I am worthy of their love and respect.

And then the war ended, and my side, South Vietnam, had lost. We lost our freedom and we lost our country. It was a scary time for everyone, except for me. I thought, *Oh my gosh, this change is what I needed!* I didn't know what it was going to look like, but I woke up and started thriving from deep inside.

Peasant Trait #6: I thrive in chaos and emergency situations. I come alive and feel very useful. For a long time, I would turn every situation into an urgent matter so that I could be strong and useful.

A year and a half after the Communists took over Vietnam, my family escaped on a tiny broken-down fishing boat. We were thirty-one of the 800,000-plus "Boat People" who fled Vietnam. We were rescued by a ship, sheltered in Japan for nine months, and then arrived in California and began our new life. Both in Japan and in the US, we were helped and assisted by members of local churches.

Peasant Trait #7: Being an underdog gets me a lot of help. So being "less than" will earn me love and support.

Peasant Trait #8: Receiving hand-me-down stuff wasn't so bad. Over time I made up a story that all the finer things in life belonged to other people. I got the second best.

For the next twenty years, I worked hard to build my life. I paid for my own college and achieved a bachelor's degree in mechanical engineering. This degree was to please my parents, to make them proud. It was also to get myself a good and solid job, even though this was not my forte. It took me seven years to complete a four-year program. I barely got through with a C+ GPA. My mother kept guilting me with her threats that she would die of old age before I graduated.

Peasant Trait #5 Reinforced: I hung on tenaciously. I worked harder and accomplished what I set out to do, even though I did not like it, and it was not right for me. (Can you see where this is heading?)

Let's talk about boys and men. When I was in high school, no boy liked me because I was an ugly and weird-looking Asian girl, an anomaly to them. In the seventies and eighties, being Asian in California was not cool or part of the mainstream. Due to my low self-esteem and lack of awareness of the social games of an American girl, I didn't know what it took to get a boy's attention. So in college I set out to land myself a boyfriend. It was easy to have men be my friends and buddies, but no one saw me as girlfriend material. This hurt me deeply.

Peasant Trait #9: I am a strong woman, but not desired by boys. So I hide myself in baggy clothes and masculine behaviors to protect myself from the deep hurt of being unseen by boys.

In my third year of college, I met a man who was nine years older than I was. I decided that he was "the one" and set out to convince him that I was his one and only. After three years I became his official girlfriend. We moved in together after college, bought a house, and got married eight years into the relationship. On our tenth wedding anniversary I asked him why he married me. He said, "Because it was Valentine's Day and I didn't know what to get you. I knew that you would be happy if I proposed. So I did." For my part, I said yes to him because he was a good man, loyal, and loving to me. And because I didn't have a better offer. Needless to say, I did not have romance, just a solid partnership and love.

Peasant Trait #10: I don't need romance. I just want to be loved. That's enough. Everything else is unnecessary and for someone else. Remember Peasant Trait #8? It got reinforced here.

The point of telling you my beginning is to show you how my *peasant* was born and reinforced over time. We all have life experiences that develop and grow our *peasant*. Our mothers, fathers, aunties, schools, and life convince us that being a good, strong *peasant* is the way to go. It will keep us safe and if we work hard enough, we will get what we want. As you can see from my story, I did achieve it all: a good job, a good husband, a house in Pleasanton, a beautiful daughter, good health... what more does a woman want? And why would I want more? Wouldn't that be selfish and greedy? Lots of people would kill for my past life. There was nothing wrong with it. Or was there?

Worksheet #1

How Did You Develop Your Peasant trait?

Write out your life story. For each part, make notes on what conclusion you made or decided about life, and yourself. These are your *peasant* traits that run your life, unconsciously, up to now.

Observe how these traits helped you and hindered you toward having the love, life, and success that you want. Follow my sample with my personal story.

If you find yourself in touch with some big stuff and not knowing how to heal or resolve, Join my community of international women who are actively moving forward with their dating life. http://www.hotlifehotlove.com/divorced-moms-dating-guide

Mai Vu Coach
www.maivucoach

www.hotlifehotlove.com

How does the Peasant date?

The *peasant* dates like she does anything else. Her view is that the world is limited. She feels there's not enough for her, that she's not good enough. She thinks things will get better if only she would improve herself. She doesn't see her own worth, and she approaches everything (running a business, forming personal relationships, dating, marriage, sex, etc.) with this mindset.

When the *peasant* dates, she looks in the mirror and sees the fat in her body, the wrinkles, the gray hairs, the imperfections, and she's thinks, *Who is going to love this?* Then she looks outside and thinks the world is a scary place. It's limiting. When she thinks about men, there are not enough of them out there. If there are, they are all taken. She won't be able to have what she wants. She looks back on her life, and thinks that she once had a shot with someone she wanted. But he turned out to be an asshole, so she makes up a story that all men are assholes and can't be trusted.

When a *peasant* is dating, she could be with the nicest guy and she would still find ways to pick him apart. He's too nice. Or he's too soft. Or he's too. . .The *peasant* will say and do everything to push him away. Then when he tries to do nice things for her, her first reaction will be, "No, I got it," "No, I don't need help." "No." It always starts with a no.

A woman can recognize when she's being overly negative. So maybe she'll try saying, "Maybe next time." "Well, maybe . . ." But "maybe" is just a fancy "no." She still doesn't let help in. She still doesn't receive him. She still nitpicks at him. She still doesn't trust him, that he will be there for her. That's where the *peasant* starts. That's why her result is that there's no man whom she wants around. They're all taken. And she'd be right. With that attitude, there is no man. If there is, he's doing something for her, and either he's too soft and wimpy or he wants something, so he's not to be trusted. Then the *peasant* finally justifies the situation with, *You know, it's just easier to be by myself. I don't want to deal with the headache.* It's such a shame. But it doesn't need to be that way.

Most of the time, the *peasant* doesn't date. She's too vulnerable and it's too scary. Most *peasants,* especially when they're moms, have a compelling reason not to do it. They put their kids first so that they can hide from dating. There are so many women who put their kids first, and this is not wholly a bad thing. But when a woman comes to me and says the following, it's a problem: "I've been single for twenty years. I put my kids first, and now they're grown and in college, and I'm looking at the rest of my life being lonely. I'm so used to my single lifestyle, and not trusting men, and not letting men come near me, and not having sex in the last twenty years. How do I fill this sense of emptiness left by my kids leaving home and not having a partner to spend time with?" Dating, relationships, and sex are very scary and foreign to this kind of woman, and it's going to take her a while to adjust to sharing her space and time with another person in an intimate way.

These women can't even fathom letting a man get close. They make up stories that what they want doesn't exist, or that the guys they are interested in want something else. Even if they tried to go out on a date with someone, they are awkward, they don't know what to do, and even if a man is into them, they will push him away. But most of what they attract is unqualified men.

I have actually had clients say things to me like, "I don't want to date another guy who doesn't have all of his teeth." I tell them, "I don't want you to date anyone who doesn't have all of his teeth, either! If that's who you're dating, please stop. Just stop." Anyway, they scare themselves with the prospect of not finding someone suitable for them, or they scare themselves with the image of their abusive ex-husband. This is the woman who does not date.

Then there are women who are dating and hurting themselves left and right. It is so scary and sad to hear their stories. They are not satisfied with the men, but they have sex when they shouldn't and/or when they don't want to. They need to get drunk. They think a good time is going on a date, getting drunk, doing it, and then hopefully he'll call. Then they wonder why he doesn't call. They tolerate all kinds of substandard treatment from the men. The guys who call are the ones they don't want, and the ones they want tend to want someone else. Men don't call them, don't treat them well, make them pay for things, and still women pine for them.

It's a vicious cycle, and these women bring all sorts of drama into their lives. If they are dating, they likely feel guilty about it. They should be at home with the kids, they are afraid of their sex, they don't know what to do with it, and then they are afraid of men, and so the dating is really clunky and awful.

One client has this pattern of dating men whose places she can't ever go to. He lives with his mother, or his son, or his sister, and she has to drop him off at the corner. I ask her, "What the hell are you doing with this type of man? Why do you even have to drive him home? What is going on here?" Different women will have different patterns play out, and they keep repeating that pattern. This is how a *peasant* dates.

Worksheet #2

Listening To Your Peasant Pain

1. What does your *peasant* want and need?

      From you?

      from The world?

      from Men?

2. What is her life story?

3. What is she afraid of?

4. How desperate does she feel? What other feelings does your peasant have besides the list in this chapter.

5. Does she know what she really really wants? If yes, what is it or what are they? If no, tell us about that.

6. And does she know how to get what she wants? What are her strategies for getting what she wants? (to be more specific, check out the Peasant Trap section below...)

7. What gets in her way?

8. What does she think of men? or Her pattern of relationships with men?

9. What is her relationship to sex in general? to her sex? her sexuality? Does she even know the difference between her sex and sexuality?

Mai Vu Coach
www.maivucoach

www.hotlifehotlove.com

What are the results of a Peasant dating?

She's in a lot of pain. The biggest result is that she's not getting the love and support that she wants and needs. If she's not dating, she lives with this constant loneliness, one she's so used to by now that she doesn't even recognize it's there, but when she touches it, it pains her deeply. This is a big truth, and it's so depressing that she just can't face it. These are the women who eat ice cream alone at night, watching television with their cats. To be clear, there is nothing wrong with watching TV, loving your pets, or eating ice cream. But when there is a habitual numbing that takes place night after night, when you're no longer engaging or trying to engage, that's a problem.

When my marriage fell apart, I moved into a one-bedroom apartment in a fourplex. In this fourplex were four single women. I swear to you, my next-door neighbor had been single for so long. She lived in a studio apartment, and it was cluttered with scrapbooking projects. She had that and her television; that was all she needed. She went to work, and she came home and crawled into her hole. The lady upstairs lived alone. She was very overweight, she took care of someone's kids in town, and that was all I saw of her. I saw her just get home and crawl into that. The other neighbor who lived above me was young and beautiful, but she was super scared and not dating either. Her mother would come over, or she would go to her mom's home nearby, and that was it.

This is how women who are not dating live, and the other women who are dating struggle. They don't think much of themselves, and they aren't living fulfilling lives. They are embarrassed and insecure, and they make compromises that they don't really want to make.

The *peasant* is petrified of her own sex. She's limited in her knowledge, and she thinks of sex as a threat. Perhaps her mother taught her that men just want things from you—they want to screw you, and they want to leave you—so she enters any relationship already suspicious of men.

Basically, the *peasant* doesn't know her own worth. She doesn't know her own beauty, she doesn't appreciate herself, and she doesn't see herself as a *princess*. Let's just be blunt about that. If she does, she thinks that the *princess* is foo-foo, unworthy, and just another spoiled diva. She doesn't really understand the world at all; she doesn't understand her power or who she is.

The *peasant* deserves to be loved, adored, and cherished, but she thinks that she has to earn others' approval; she has to prove that she is good enough, smart enough, savvy enough, pretty enough, etc. And yet when she looks in the mirror, she doesn't see herself as enough. Imagine how she dates!

This is what's missing for nearly all women on this planet: we miss out on being loved, adored, and cherished. This is so important. We think we can do without that, and that's why our lives run dry. That's why we're so exhausted, so lonely, so scared, and that's why we're so dissatisfied with our relationships. Because we don't know what it takes to have that, and to cultivate that.

Worksheet #3

Are You Dating Like A Peasant?

When it comes to dating... [Check All that Apply:]

❑ I think I am too old, fat, or unattractive to get a man's attention
❑ I try to give the guy a chance, but always end up disappointed
❑ I tend to attract men who are not available
❑ The men i meet don't bring me to their home
❑ I get frustrated that all men want sex from me
❑ I need to have a connection before anything can happen
❑ I fret about what to wear and how I look when I go out on a date
❑ I don't trust men
❑ I worry about what my family and/or friends will think
❑ I avoid it all cost
❑ I am afraid of attracting men i don't want
❑ I can't fit it into my schedule
❑ I am too set in my ways, I have been living alone for too long
❑ I am tired, I just want to find THE ONE
❑ I don't want to date, I just want a committed relationship
❑ I am afraid I will be disappointed again
❑ I keep comparing the new guy with my ex or past significant relationship
❑ I don't want to play game, i just want to be appreciated for who I am
❑ Appearance is important to me (no bald men, etc...)
❑ I am completely bored with my boyfriend
❑ I don't see any quality men around
❑ I think I have to work hard to find the one
❑ I expect to be treated a certain way and I am not going to lower my standard
❑ It's not fair that my ex is having fun and dating, and I am not
❑ It has been so long, I don't know where to begin
❑ I really don't need a man in my life
❑ It's easier to be with my cat

Mai Vu Coach
www.maivucoach

What is the Peasant's role?

The *peasant's* role is to handle all the pieces of an ordinary life. While there are a lot of details to juggle and a lot of mundane tasks to do every day, a *peasant's* role should actually be very small. She should drive the car, put on clothes, put on makeup, do the physical things, the small things.

Unfortunately, most of the time our *peasant* has taken on everything. She tries to build relationships, get love, be successful, be an inspirational leader, and change the world, all from the *peasant* place. This is too much for her to handle.

The *peasant* comes with a set of skills that are very valuable, and she wants to keep them. Her skills are practicality, physicality, and making things happen. We don't want to get rid of any of that. Without a *peasant,* dishes don't get done, laundry doesn't get washed, and children don't get raised. Those things just don't happen. We need the Peasant. But we don't need her to be active 100 percent of the time.

CHAPTER TWO

The Princess

Let's talk about the Princess. Who is she?

The *princess* part of us knows her birthright, knows that she is worthy of love, that she is worthy of being taken care of. Safety and security are no longer enough; she needs more, and she cannot live without it. No compromises. She graces the world with her beauty, her generosity, and her love. She elevates people around her into their grace, joy, and ease. When a *princess* is around, she transforms the space and makes everything easier, softer, and more elegant.

In the old days, and even now, princesses were in a very precarious position. They were born into privilege, and were groomed to be royalty, but they were pawns in the complex game of kingdom building. They had no positional power like a queen did. They were compromised into terrible situations, where they had to marry men who easily became their abusers. All they had was their grace, beauty, and vulnerability to sway kings and princes into taking action on their behalf. Some came out alive and lived long enough to be queens, while other princesses were consumed by their circumstances.

Worksheet #4

Discovering Your Princess

Your *princess* is the part of you who has full compassion and love for where you are at the moment. She knows how you must be treated in order for you to be happy and satisfied. What ever the situation is ask yourself:

What does my *peasant* think about this situation? List out all of her fears, concerns, and worries.

in Dating and Relationship, Ask:
What is my *peasant* tolerating?

Then ask yourself:
What does my *princess* want? List out as honestly as you can what you truly want, no matter how unrealistic, impossible, your wants might be.

Follow it up with a simple...
What else does my *princess* want? This is really important to do, to get to the real truth. Ask this question several times, until you break out into a big smile and your eyes light up with possibilities.

Especially for Dating and Relationship, Ask:
What does my *princess* see in this guy? What's lacking? What's here that she likes? What more does she want?

Note: Don't be discouraged if you don't know what your *princess* wants at first. Many people are so out of touch with what they want, they can only name what they don't want or afraid of. If that is the case for you, keep asking yourself that question: What does my Princess want? and let the answers come to you.

Finally if the answers do not come, after several days of asking yourself that question, this is an indication of a few things:
Your *peasant* is really stuck and she needs more healing and love than you are prepared to give to her. Another word she has been abused for so long, she can't get out of your way.

You don't trust your *princess*'s whispers so you can't hear her. Or that you heard it, but you discounted it to be nothing.

Either way, you owe yourself a conversation with me.

Mai Vu Coach
www.maivucoach

How do you know your Princess self?

Here is an easy demonstration to help you begin to reconnect to her. When you walk into a dirty, dingy motel, is there a part of you that immediately knows that this is gross and that you don't belong there, even if you have only forty dollars to your name? The reverse is true, too. When you walk into a beautiful, first-class hotel room, is there a part of you who feels like, "Now this is more like it. I am home at last! This is how my life should be." That's your *princess* talking to you.

The *princess* knows where she belongs and how she should be treated. Most of the time we don't consult with her because the *peasant* is so afraid of what she has to say. The *peasant* is too busy compromising and making do with less, while the *princess* knows whether the situation—from men, to work, to shopping, to how others treat her—is up to her standards. Your *princess* part knows where you should be in life, and she won't lie. The *peasant* will cheat and lie to herself, then get mad that she settled for so little. Or she will be mad that people around her treat her so badly.

Listening to Your Princess

For one day, practice moving only when you are happy and satisfied and things are to your liking. If you don't like something, just say to yourself, "No, I don't like it; it's not to my liking." See what happens when you assert yourself.

Most of the time, we are out of touch with our *princess*. We don't trust this part of ourselves; we make this part of ourselves wrong. We lock her up, and some women even kill off the *princess* in order to protect the *peasant*. I know that for myself, having been born in the middle of a war, I received plenty of education on how to be a *peasant* and survive. My *peasant* is very proud.

There's a level of pride and satisfaction that accompanies identifying with the *peasant*. However, too much of that has us always surviving, always working so hard, always proving ourselves, and running ourselves into the ground in the process. If we could surrender and trust that our *princess* knows, and that she won't move until she has it the way she wants, life would be so much better.

I look at my daughter. Luckily, knowing what I now know, I haven't killed off her *princess*. I really help her to understand her 3Ps™ and work with them. Ever since she was a baby, my daughter naturally doesn't moved toward something if she doesn't like it. She will just stand there until everything around her changes. Guess what? Things did change to accommodate her needs. She did not budge until it felt right to her. Now, I could have been one of the typical moms whose aim was to make my daughter conform so that she didn't inconvenience others. Or I could have been a Tiger Mom whose goal was to dominate my child so that she would do as I said for "her" own good. These are all different forms of being a *peasant* mom. I could have chastised her, beat her down, and made her change her ways to fit the expectations of those around her. That's how we unconsciously create *peasant*s out of our girls, and kill of their *princess* selves. I did not do that. I listened to her, trusted her, and followed her lead. My daughter was right ninety percent of the time.

Here is a different example. One of my clients bought herself a beautiful, brand-new home that cost over a million dollars. Her dishwasher did not work. She spent two weeks trying to get the builder, the contractor, the sales office, even the manufacturer of the dishwasher to fix the problem. Everyone was pointing fingers at the other person to correct the situation. My client was livid. She came on the call frustrated and angry. I gave her a *princess* trick to try. She did not have to get mad and yell. All she had to do was simply say, "I am not happy," and then stop talking. Stop moving forward. Stop compromising. Stay there until the other person offers a better solution. My client practiced it right away. After a long silence, the person on the other end said, "You are right. I will come out personally and take care of it tomorrow morning." That was a hoot!

What's funny is that when the *princess* part of us is not happy, nobody is happy. When she is happy, the world is right again. Everyone feels better. By making the *princess* happy, the people involved actually get uplifted to the *princess* level. Men become heroes or *king*s. Other *peasant* women feel better, too, because they get to serve and solve a big problem to make the *princess* happy again.

The *peasant* is busy working hard and doesn't trust the *princess*, but if she can trust just a little bit and watch how the *princess* works, it's quite beautiful. Magic and miracles happen in this place. We attract the best to ourselves.

The *princess* way works, and it's really hard to surrender and trust that we can live by the *princess* approach. The *peasant* has a thousand reasons not to trust: *Yeah, but Mai, you don't understand...I don't have the money to do that...It happened for her, but that would never work for me... Yeah, but I'm old and I can't compete with those younger chicks...Yeah, but I have kids...* I say, *I totally understand your fears and doubt. And if you would try it, you would be amazed at what would happen for you.*

Our *peasant* stays limited in her thinking, and she doesn't think she's worth it. The *princess* knows she's worth it. She knows what is not right, and she will wait until things become right.

When we allow our *princess* to thrive along with our *peasant* and our *priestess*, we gain the beauty, love, benevolence, and joy of the *princess* to uplift and add magic to the *peasant*'s hard work and the *priestess's* wisdom. We are soft and beautiful, yet competent and dependable, while powerfully leading ourselves forward. This is what we want.

Why the Princess archetype, and not a Queen?

I love that question. I've seen what people have done with the queen archetype, and it's ugly. To me, a queen is a glorified *peasant*. She's a *peasant* with power and even more responsibility. Being a *princess* is an art. The *princess* doesn't have any positional power; she is a pawn whom the king and queen use to create peace in the kingdom. The *princess* gets put in the most precarious of positions. She gets married off to someone and she has no choice in the matter. The only things she has are her sweetness, her beauty, and her vulnerability. Those are her weapons. She has to learn to win the world over with her essence, her beauty, her belief in herself, and her own self-worth, as well as her vulnerability. That's all she's got.

Yet princesses have been able to change the world. Remember Princess Diana of Wales? Her presence continues to win over our hearts. She raised so much money and support for whatever cause she stood for. The whole world feels elevated whenever we see her images. And her journey as the Princess of Wales was not easy. It even ended in death. However, her *princess* essence continues to intrigue and inspire us. That's the power of a *princess*. I see women who want to go straight from *peasant* to queen. All they do is take their baggage, put a bunch of bling on it, and become more demanding and harsh (although they call it "confidence"). They haven't learned to soften and access their vulnerable selves, to access their trust; they've just learned how to be more flamboyantly demanding. That's why I don't use the queen metaphor.

How does the Princess date?

The *princess* has so much more fun with dating than the *peasant* does. Men come from all over to help her. The *peasant* dates one man after another. She pines over a man. She says no to everyone else, and she's stuck with the one. The *princess* is truly like the fairy tale princess. Men from all over try to win a date with her. They bring her amazing things, they adore her, and they fight to win her attention.

The *princess* does only things that please her. The *princess's* job is to trust, surrender, open up, and let love in. She has amazing sex, and she doesn't do things to please the man; she is the one being pleased. Yet in so doing, she pleases her man. This is a paradox that a *peasant* has a hard time to understand. The *peasant* will do things to please a man so that it's tit for tat: "If he does this, I have to do that." The *princess* simply receives. This makes the man feel like a superhero. He feels like the greatest lover on the planet, and he gets better and better at serving her, bringing her to orgasm, and bringing her joy. She doesn't have to compromise herself.

What is the Princess's pain? What is her pleasure?

A reminder that we need a balance among all 3Ps™. When a woman is mostly *princess*, with very little *peasant* or *priestess*, she is beautiful, soft, fun, and even sexy. But she has a hard time getting practical things done. Life's chores, like building a business, are stalled because she does not have her *peasant* to do the hard work and the *priestess* to guide the way. She has to be dependent financially on another person. Over time, she may be a *princess* on the outside, but without a competent *peasant* and a powerful *priestess* guiding her, she is an unhappy mess inside. She will be a kept woman. Her *princess* will devolve into a sad and frustrated *peasant* woman who doesn't want to stay and be dependent. Yet she can't leave because she is ill-equipped to handle the financial burden of life.

If the *princess* is the only strong force of the three parts, she doesn't have enough oomph, enough power. Sometimes you need your *priestess*, and sometimes you need your *peasant* to deal with other *peasant*s in the world.

You know that there are bad men out there. There are men who are on a different journey. The *princess* allows herself to be vulnerable and all-loving, and she receives most everyone. Most of the time, she attracts only wonderful beings into her life because that is her vibration. There are times when you have to learn about your own strength and power. You might find yourself in situations beyond what your *princess* can do for you. So you need your *priestess* to have strong-enough boundaries and power to keep you safe.

In the beginning, men like the challenge of taking care of a *princess*. That is the hard truth about dating. Men don't really want a *peasant*, and you don't want to be a *peasant* in a relationship, anyway. As much as men will deny this, all men want a *princess* to take care of. It makes them feel like a hero, it makes them feel powerful; it makes them feel like they are bringing a lot to the table. When they are faced with another *peasant*, they actually become lazy. It feeds their *peasant*, and it has them do less. Over time, they lose themselves and their power. Their lazy selves will say, "Oh yeah, I'll take a *peasant* instead of a *princess*. I don't want to have to work that hard for a woman."

Those men are lying. All men aspire to have a *princess*, someone they feel so proud to be with and for whom they will do anything. That's what makes a man great. That's the result; it's a great match. When you step into your *princess,* you allow the man to be his greatest self. When you step into the *peasant*, you're competing with him or you become his caretaker.

What is the Princess's role?

The *princess*'s role is to love unconditionally. Love when everything else around you says, "Don't! You should protect yourself." The *princess* shows us how to be vulnerable, and she wins the world over with her vulnerability. The *princess* holds magic, vulnerability, and unconditional love. (While all three parts, *peasant*, *princess*, and *priestess*, have love in them, they express it differently.)

The job of the *princess* is to know your birthright, to know what you truly want inside. If every woman knows what she wants at every moment of the day, she would not have the life she has. The problem is that the *peasant* compromises. This is how we get into the messes we do. If you are always in touch with what you want, and you're always moving toward what you want, your life is always great. This is what I call a HotLifeHotLove™.

How do you cultivate your inner Princess?

First, you need to heal your *peasant*. If we try to cultivate the *princess* before healing the *peasant*, the *peasant* is going to be really pissed off. She's going to feel unappreciated and replaced, and she's going to retaliate: *I got you this far with my hard work and dedication. Now you took on a*

*coach and you're all princess this and princess that. You're ditching me?
Well, fuck you. Go do the dishes yourself, princess so-and-so!* (Can you
just hear your *peasant* screaming inside?)

The *peasant* gets really mad because she just wants to be loved. She
works so hard for love, and if she isn't appreciated, she will not step aside
and let you have your *princess*. You cannot access your *princess* until you
see your *peasant*, appreciate her, and love her like crazy. When you do
that, your *princess* naturally comes out.

I spend 75 percent of my time with clients healing and loving and
showing them how to love and take care of their *peasant*. Once we've
accomplished that, the rest is much easier. Suddenly, they're wanting
more. They're like, "Gosh, Mai, now show me how to be a *princess* all
day long." I say, "Okay, that's the easy part. You resisting your *princess*—
that's the harder part."

Women can't get to sex either until we heal the *peasant*'s pain. Until
we make it safe for her, and love her so that she knows that her *princess*
and *priestess* are with her. Then she can inch her way out and surrender
to, "Okay, now let's talk about sex. I'm ready." It can take a long time to
get to this point. With a coach, it can take six months to a year. For women
who are working on these issues by themselves, I'm sad to say that most
end up hurting their *peasant*s more. They simply do not know how to
heal the *peasant*. They get really impatient with themselves. Their *peasant*
ends up compromising herself and adding more shame and resistance in
the process.

When you have love and community and guidance, it's super easy.
I mean, you should see the brilliant faces of my clients, the light in their
eyes, and the joy that's coming back into their lives after a few months of
work.

CHAPTER THREE

The Priestess

We've talked about the Peasant and the Princess. Now, who is the Priestess?

I think "Priestess" is a word that, until now, we've been very afraid of. It has a connotation. Our *priestess* is this part inside ourselves that is so powerful, so all knowing, as if she has wisdom from lifetimes ago. She also has insight for humanity that's far-reaching, like looking into the future and seeing where humanity needs to be going. She holds purpose. She has power, true power, and she exerts clarity and freedom. The Priestess is that voice inside that is very quiet, but very clear. This voice tells you the truth. Surrender to the deep wisdom and guidance of the *priestess*, no matter how scary it may be. Her perspective will allow you to be fully in your own power, comfortable in your own skin, fully self-expressed, and totally independent.

The *princess* holds love, generosity, softness, and vulnerability. The *priestess* holds power, clarity, freedom, inspiration, and direction. The *priestess* knows. She works in mysterious ways. The majority of us don't normally live through our *priestess,* but some do. Because the *priestess* is so powerful, her truths scare us and intimidate others around us.

I remember when I was around ten years old, I was a little, itty-bitty thing. I would walk through a typical family gathering at my aunt and uncle's house, and my aunt or uncle would look at me quizzically. Sometimes they would blurt out, "That child, she knows something. I am afraid of her." I'm thinking, 'What are you talking about? How am I scary? I'm just a kid.' I believe that even back then, I had some access to my *priestess* self, and my family could pick up on that energy.

We all have this *priestess* self, though her influence can be more prevalent in some people than in others. Many healers and coaches, for example, have strong *priestess* energy, like they're tapping into something. They have a calling, and they go for it. They do their work in life from that *priestess* calling, despite the *peasant*'s voice rattling inside their head, *I don't know what I'm doing. Oh my gosh, am I good enough yet?* Yet they're driven toward a purpose. The problem with most healers is that they are so engrossed in the *priestess* land that they don't know how to tend to their *peasant*, or they are impatient with their *peasant*. This lack of care for the *peasant* impedes their success in their business, and sometimes blocks them from truly doing their work. It's important to know how to integrate the 3Ps™.

Jane Goodall is a great example of a *priestess*. She was called to study the apes and to be among them. Then she discovered something so much bigger than what humanity was aware of. She chose to stay in the jungle; she worked and did her thing. She gained amazing wisdom and access to knowledge that she brought back to the world. You can feel it when you look at her. She knew her work in the world and she went for it, societal norms be damned. She didn't care about fitting in. She found her freedom. She was free to live her life however she saw fit. The *peasant* is all tied up with obligations, responsibilities, shame, and worthiness issues, while Jane just followed her own calling and direction.

Madeleine Albright is another super *priestess*. I see her as both *peasant* and *priestess*—hardworking, competent, powerful. She used to be out there directing men and generals, making a huge impact in the world. But she's not loved. She's not remembered as a woman. She was not approachable. She was just strong, competent, and fierce. That's what happens when you're all *priestess* and *peasant* but not enough *princess*. The Princess is there to soften you up, to really make yourself accessible so that the world will love you.

I see Oprah as a nice combination of all three parts. She was a super *peasant* in her early years in Chicago. Back then she was just starting to find her place in the world. She worked really hard and overcame lots of obstacles (including her childhood) to achieve what she did. When she got her own show, she was pressured to do it certain ways. But over time, she had a calling and she followed it, moving toward her own vision for her show. She was very strong in her *peasant*, and her *priestess* was guiding her with every brave decision she made.

In the beginning, there was not much *princess* essence in Oprah. Oprah developed her *princess* right in front of us. Her journey with her weight was a huge demonstration of her learning to love herself as-is. As she gained and lost weight, with every confession and every tear, her *peasant* softened and her *princess* came out. Now you can see her *princess* grace in everything she does. Her branding is super-loving, soft, and beautiful. We all can see the Oprah essence and impact. The energy that Oprah puts out elevates women and allows millions of tired and overwhelmed *peasant*s around the world to approach her. This is the power of leading with your *princess* and *peasant*.

Her latest move in the last five or six years, when she ended *The Oprah Winfrey Show* and created the Oprah Winfrey Network, or OWN, was driven by her integrated 3Ps™. It took guts. She wanted more freedom, more accessibility, a bigger reach. She's here to do work in the world, so off she went. This winning combination of *peasant*, *princess*, and *priestess* has made Oprah the success she is today. Her *priestess* is at the helm, with her wisdom and clarity, while her *princess* adds softness, beauty, love, heart, and soul. Her *peasant* follows with countless hours of hard work, difficult negotiations, travels, etc. When all 3P™s are working together, with the *priestess* and *princess* leading the way and the *peasant* being healthy and whole, a woman can have global reach like Oprah.

Worksheet #5

Discovering Your Priestess

Your *priestess* voice can be very quiet or very loud, depending on how long you have tolerated a situation. When your *priestess* is speaking, it is very clear, and succinct. It usually sounds like "do this" or "Not acceptable" or "That's right" Unfortunately, most of the time your *peasant's* fearful self will interfere with your *priestess* instruction, she muddy up the reception, and you end up struggling with a dilemma.

Therefore, when you find yourself in a dilemma or a struggle ask yourself:
If I am not afraid, what would I do here?

What is UNACCEPTABLE here?

What is MOST important here?

What am I avoiding?

What am I trying to say, but am too afraid to say it?

And when it comes to dating, Ask yourself:
What do I really see in this person? (go with your guts, your intuition, learn to trust it.)

How powerful or self-authorized do I feel in this relationship so far?

What do I want that I have not spoken?

Does your *priestess* even want to be here?

Remember:
Your *priestess* is about freedom, full self-expression and full right to be who you are and to do what you are meant to do in this lifetime.

If you skip pass your *princess*, and just rely on your *peasant* and *priestess* alone, you may accomplish lots of big things, command respect, but not many people will enjoy being around you. That makes dating not much fun at all.

Mai Vu Coach
www.maivucoach

---

www.hotlifehotlove.com

How does the Priestess date?

The *priestess* part of ourselves is so awesome. I don't think a *priestess* really dates. This is much bigger than most women can fathom. Just imagine a situation where you feel fully empowered and you're not afraid of men, of yourself, of sex, of your body. You never wonder whether you're good enough—basically, all the things your *peasant is* concerned about when it comes to dating. The *priestess* is super connected to her sexuality. She has no shame about her desires or decision to leave or stay. She is free to roam the country, as they say. When she selects a man, it's because she wants to eat him up, devour him, enjoy him, and satisfy herself. She doesn't need a relationship. She doesn't need to have a long-term engagement. She doesn't need a wedding ring on her finger to prove that she's somebody. She just wants to experience, enjoy, and bring out her full power and the other person's full power. Everything is satiated with satisfaction. When the *priestess* is done having sex, everyone is exhausted. Spent. But both partners are left wondering, *When can we go again?*

It's a place of full freedom that most of us don't let ourselves get to. We get all tripped up about everything here. To be honest, most women are not ready for their *priestess*. They're super scared, and they're tied down with religious constraints and "b.s." conditioning in the head. Another word: Our *peasant* conditioning prevents us from accessing our *priestess*. Our *peasant* is afraid of wrecking everything that she worked so hard to earn. When she looks at the *priestess's* way, she cannot fathom giving up what she has to trade for that freedom and full self-expression. In the *peasant*'s mindset, it is a trade-off, not an integration. The *peasant* has a hard time imagine that she can have it all. It will cost too much.

We must work on undoing some of this conditioning so that we can access our *priestess'* guidance and wisdom. We need her back desperately so that we can do our work in the world.

Does the Priestess ever experience pain?

Yes. The *priestess* can be very lonely. People can misunderstand her tremendously. When a woman is growing her *priestess*, she goes through a phase where she's like a teenager—rebellious because she doesn't really understand her full power yet. What's more, nobody has explained to her what's going on, or shown her how to work with her power. There are very few models of *priestesses* in our everyday world. We are mostly surrounded by *peasant*s. Furthermore, society has a long history of killing *priestesses* because they are powerful and we don't understand or are afraid of that power. We cannot be controlled when we are in touch with our *priestess* power, so our parents have tried to kill our *priestess*. Our church has done the same. So have our schools, government, boyfriends, husbands, fathers, sisters… They don't want us to be a *priestess* because we would out-think them.

Up to now, most people do not support the *priestess*. We all love the *princess*; *princesses* are easier to love. We have had a whole history of burning women at the stake, beheading them, calling them witches, putting them away, all because the *priestess* was coming out and providing guidance. Yes, the pain of the *priestess* is embedded in our DNA over several lifetimes. That's why we're so afraid of our power. Every woman (and I think every man, too) has this fear of, *If I am too much, they'll kill me. If I make waves, it won't be welcomed, and I will be thrown out of the community.*

Right now, most of us are in *peasant* mode and we shove the *peasant* into the world. We do everything from the *peasant* mode. No wonder we're so disempowered, so limited in our success, and so sucky in love.

If we could see that, all women would enter the room as a *princess* first. You know you're beautiful, you know you're worthy, you know you're capable, you know where you belong. Awesome. You go in as a *princess* first, and your *priestess* is right behind her. You have an inner strength. You have clarity, so you can speak to anybody who tries to compromise you at any moment in the most loving and generous way. But there's a clear direction of where you need to be, what you need to be doing at every given moment.

The *priestess* is there governing, making sure everything is safe and going in the right direction. Then the *peasant* is free to do all her *peasant* stuff—cook, clean, etc.—and she doesn't have to worry. She doesn't have to be so scared. She doesn't have to be so alone in the world anymore.

What is the Priestess's role?

The *priestess* holds our freedom, our power, our sense of safety, and our purpose in the world. When a woman has access to her *priestess*, she has her own internal guidance. She hears a larger calling and purpose than just her need to pay the bills. Because the *priestess* is self-directed, she does not look elsewhere for approval or acceptance, and she feels free to do or be what she wants. She generates her own sense of well-being and safety in everyday life.

How do you cultivate your Priestess?

To be honest, most women are so depleted that they can't get to the *priestess*. But that's not going to be us. First, you have to know your *peasant*. As your *peasant* softens, your *princess* will come out and allow you to elevate yourself and reach a more satisfied place in life. You are filled with love, softness, community, acceptance, and joy. When you refuel your tank, you will radiate with love. Naturally, your *priestess* will come out. You will feel ready for a larger calling, something like, "Okay, now we are ready to take life forward. We're ready to be a productive citizen and a leader in this world. We're ready to step into power and guide others, and this is where we need to go."

What normally happens to a woman in real life is that she is a hard-working *peasant*, busy minding her own business, trying to keep up with her life. Then she gets a little calling from her *priestess* intuition to do something greater, perhaps to right a wrong or to lead a cause. Innocently, she goes straight from her already tired and overwhelmed *peasant* state to taking on a humongous *priestess* calling. True to form, she takes on the cause with no replenishment, no support. She thinks she can do it herself. All she has to do is work harder. She is completely out of touch with her *princess* self. Even though she is taking on a big task, she thinks very little of herself. She does not feel deserving enough for help or support. So her *peasant* self is trying to mobilize the world to get behind her cause, to accomplish her *priestess* agenda. But she has zero *princess* softness, beauty, and inspiration. She is all alone. She is doomed.

Many nonprofit female leaders embody this description. They are Wonder Women who are drained and unkempt because they are doing too much with very little self-care and support. Most likely, she doesn't have a man to love and support her. She is either single or unhappily married. Over time, her depletion becomes resentment, and she alienates people with her anger and short temper. She continues to work harder and yet she's not getting what she wants. Her body breaks down. She cannot receive any success, even if it comes her way.

Once you know how to love and tend to your *peasant*'s needs, how to have better conversations with yourself through your *princess*, you can have an intimate relationship with your *priestess*. This is what I teach my clients to do.

Tending to your *peasant* is not so hard. However, this is a difficult first step for most women to take because they are really hurt and angry. They are negative and disbelieving. First, they will resist: "Don't you call me a *peasant*! You don't know what I've been through," or "*princess*? What the hell is that?" Just the word "*princess*" can trigger so much anger. That's because the *peasant* doesn't understand that when I use the word "*peasant*," I use it with love, honor, and the utmost respect. I love my *peasant*. Without her, nothing gets done. The *princess*, on the other hand, is NOT a passive, pretty, and spoiled brat. She is joyous, warm, generous, loving, and magnetic.

You need to love and honor your *peasant*'s contribution. When she's scared, you need to take care of that fear so that she doesn't have to create negative things in the world to get your attention. This is how you avoid having drama in your life. When something close to drama happens, ask yourself, "Okay, what is going on here that I need to heal, that I need to love, that I need to forgive, so that it's smooth and easy again?" That's your *princess* talking. She is saying, "How can I help? How can I love you? Let me help you." That's the kind of conversation you want to have, not the old conversations that sounded like, "What is wrong with me? Why am I still doing this? Am I stupid?" Those kinds of conversations will be long gone once you're able to soothe your *peasant* with your *princess.*

When the *peasant* softens, magic and miracles do happen. The *priestess* voice will come to the surface to guide you, and you'll be in a position to listen and to act. Love does come. Support is right in front of you all the time. All you have to do is ask for help. Did you know that you're entitled to receive help all the time?

From this softer place, where your *peasant* and *princess* are working together, you are ready to bring your *priestess* into the picture. Together, all 3Ps™ will rock the world and have so much fun while enjoying success and love.

CHAPTER FOUR

Before You Date . . .

I know you're eager to get into "the good stuff," the dating stuff, but there are a few things we need to square away before you're ready for that. We've uncovered your *peasant, princess,* and *priestess,* and we've done a little bit of work on healing them and enabling them to fulfill their own roles and to work together to help you achieve wholeness. While healing yourself is some of the most important work you'll do, as a divorced parent you also have some other factors to consider that make dating a little more complicated than it already is: your kids, your work, and your ex. In this chapter, we'll discuss how you can get clear on these aspects of your life so that when the time comes you're ready to get back out there and date; you're covered.

How do we date differently and better?

The dating game starts within you, so there is all this healing and structure to work on. Have you ever started a new project at work and had a team member want to jump right into things without forming a plan? Because planning takes too long and removes all the fun? More often than not, about a third of the way into the project, they hit a roadblock. They have questions. And then it takes them a lot longer to undo what they started, or, at worst, they have to give up completely and start from the beginning. The same goes for dating.

If you don't want to do your personal work and want to jump into dating right away, you can do that. There are many men out there whom you can go out with, but what you end up discovering is that you're repeating patterns, you're getting hurt, and you're going to end up repeating every emotional wound you've had up to that point. Finally, you'll just throw up your hands and say, "Forget it." Or maybe you meet someone, fall in love, get married, and then five, ten years later, you look at your partner and think, *Oh my gosh, I'm bored.* But you don't dare upset the relationship, so it's more of the same.

You have to spend time doing your personal work beforehand. If you haven't done so already, start learning about your *peasant*. Practice being a *princess*. Meet your *priestess*. Get to know who you are and what you want. This doesn't take as much time as you might think—you just need to focus and give yourself some space and privacy to think. When people work with me, it usually takes between three and six months to heal the *peasant* and access the *princess*. As you heal your *peasant*, you'll get to know your *princess*. *Boom.* Immediately, men are showing up and it's like, "Oh my God, who knew there are so many great men are out there!" You don't have to do online dating. You don't have to work so hard at finding love.

I have clients from the U.S. and Sweden who are hard, drawn out, mentally exhausted, and jaded. Even in these tough cases, once they start getting to know what their *peasant* wants, listening to their *peasant*'s story, learning to hear themselves, after just two months, five out of seven of them are dating men they're really excited about. They're doing their personal work. Magic and miracles are showing up in front of them. You don't need to go out and search for anything; just let things come to you and work on maintaining a balanced head (your *peasant),* a wide-open heart (your *princess*), and a "no-shame' groin (your *priestess*).

Your Kids

Let's talk about raising children for a minute.

That is my favorite topic! As much as I love talking about relationships, raising children is the most important thing. I saw this nature documentary that said that in the animal kingdom if the female species is weak, the species will die out. If the female is weak, she can't breed. And if she is somehow able to have a baby, she can't protect it, if she fails to protect herself. I believe the same thing goes for the human species.

I mentioned earlier that I do a lot of my work in Sweden, which I love. Sweden is a very beautiful and fascinating country. It is consistently named one of the top ten happiest countries every year, but in my experience, I encounter many women who are on anti-depressants or who take sick leave because they cannot work anymore. Their minds are unstable and their bodies are breaking down. Through my one-on-one conversations I learned that as a society, Sweden believes in equality between men and women. This, on the whole, is a very good thing. But within this philosophy is the implication that women should not go to their *princess or priestess* realm. They want their women to be equal to men almost to the point of androgyny or asexuality. Women are not encouraged to engage their *princess* characteristics. They are not encouraged to be seen as beautiful. There is very little flirting between men and women. Furthermore, being soft and vulnerable is not valued. The women are starving for their *princess* self because of it. They are unstable and tired. They overwhelm themselves with responsibilities and duties and their children can feel this stress in the family.

If a mother is weak, she is not able to fully be there for her children. This is why I am doing the work that I do. When we women know our own worth, who we are, and why we are here, when we know how to be strong yet maintain our softness and our vulnerability, we don't kill our daughter's *princesses* and turn them into hard-core *peasants*. It's so easy for a mom to unknowingly pass on her *peasant* traits to her daughter or son with her fears, her limited thinking, her judgment of men, her worries about money, and so on. Mothers are committed to keeping their children safe in the world. Most *peasant* mothers do not feel safe in the world. We see the world as a scary place; life is hard, and you must work hard to get what you want. We see our children as helpless, weak beings who need our protection, so we exhaust ourselves with overprotection, doing things for them and sheltering them from what we consider the "harsh life." The *peasant* mom mindset thinks this is good mothering. *Peasant* moms tend to forget that children are smart and resilient; they will know or find their way if we trust them and help them navigate the world by reminding them of their birthright and innate power and wisdom. When we protect our children so much that we crush their spirits, or, alternatively, smother them with our love because we are too insecure to live our lives, we will lead them to our *peasant* way instead of the *princess* (or *prince/king*) and *priestess* way.

It's important to teach your children about the three parts of themselves as soon as you can. The *peasant* is a valuable aspect of the personality, as are the *princess* and *priestess* (or *prince/king* and *magician*). Teach your kids about the virtues of the *peasant*: hard work, dedication, respect, giving back, responsibility. Without the *peasant* influence, you have privilege (the *princess*) without wisdom (*priestess*), which is a very scary thing. The reverse is also true; if you teach them about hard work but with no sense of their birthright or their power, they will grow up disempowered and reach for very little in life.

Also look out for patterns or cycles of behavior that get passed on from generation to generation. If you are raising a child who grows up to respect others, respect themselves, and respect you, and they feel free to respect their voice and tell you what they want, you did a great job. You have helped them get the 3Ps™ together. Congratulations. If you are doing that and you are exhausted yourself, you have given too much. This is easy to do as a parent. Remember that for you to be there for your kids, you must be healthy and whole yourself.

Kids learn from us how to be in the world, so first do everything you can to educate yourself, forgive yourself, learn how to take care of your *peasant*, and learn how to have compassion for yourself. Then you can help your children have compassion for and trust themselves.

Trust is huge when it comes to parenting. I don't know how, but my daughter knows that there is a line she cannot cross, and that line is there to support her. She knows that I love her, and we have respect for each other. It's all energetic. She has a choice to leave if it's what she wants. I give a lot to her, and I ask a lot from her in return. What I ask of her is a full investment to be in relationship with me. This is something I don't see a lot of other mothers do.

I'm surprised to see how many mothers do not insist that their children be good to them. It's almost like the children are doing their parents a favor when they treat them well. But the parents do not say, "Wait a minute, that is not acceptable to me." Children should treat us with respect because this is how they learn to respect themselves. They should learn this from a young age. It is important that we hold our power as well as softness and vulnerability in our relationships with our children. Whatever we are going through, we must allow them to see our own vulnerable journey with ourselves. When they can see our struggles and failures as life unfolds, they have access to us and we have access to them.

Built on that deep relationship is the practicality of life: they need to do the dishes, they need to be home when they say they'll be home, and they need to make sound decisions that respect them and us. But they don't have to do these things to earn love from us, to earn worthiness of life. They need to do these things so that they can take good care of themselves in the future. They have to learn now.

There is a lot to say when it comes to parenting from the 3Ps™. The conversations we should be having with our children are so different from the conversations parents are having with their children right now. Let's talk about sex, for example. We approach the topic of sex from the *peasant* perspective: sex is shameful, an embarrassment. It belongs to you and it should be kept behind closed doors. We think this is wisdom we are passing on to our children, but it's misguided. We don't show our children our bodies. We are shy and embarrassed, which sends the message to our young children that they should be ashamed and embarrassed of their own bodies, too.

Then we hide our sexual self from them, thinking that this is inappropriate. What is the big deal about parents having sex? We can't have sex in front of our babies, and when they get older we shut the door, pretending that sex is non-existent. Mom cannot make a sound. Why? When our children are younger, sex does not exist, but once a child reaches a certain age, it suddenly *does* exist and we are supposed to have a conversation about it. This is a one-time event, and by the time we sit down to talk, the child has gone through years of embarrassment surrounding sex. We have lost the chance to instill a healthy attitude about sex.

On my daughter's eighth birthday, I took her and her friend out for dinner. As we were enjoying our meal, my daughter's friend whispered to her, "May I ask her?"

"Ask me what?" I said.

And then she asked me about sex.

"My parents never talk to me about sex," the friend said.

"Well, what have your parents said when you've asked them about it?" I asked.

She replied that her dad told her to talk to her mom. When she talked to her mom, her response was, "Sex is a wonderful thing and you should wait until you are older and married." I asked her what she thought about their answers. She said she was disappointed that they were not being real with her. She just knew that there was more to sex than what they were telling her. And that she wished they would be straight to her. My heart broke hearing that.

We mess things up because we are not listening and not being real with our kids. We confuse them, and they end up not trusting themselves. Then they lose their voice. Around eight years old, a girl will lose her voice. She will doubt herself and no longer trust that she can make the right decisions.

I don't understand why we assume that our children wouldn't understand sex, love, and relationships. Of course they don't need to know everything from day one, but I think we treat them like they don't know anything when they do. They know from the moment they come out of our body. They look at us and they can feel our energy. Without a word they know what we know and what we don't, what we have resolved and what we haven't.

So, knowing this, let's let the *princess* teach our children about sex, about pleasure, about trusting our bodies, about listening to ourselves, about knowing what we really want in this moment. Every time and in every given moment the *princess* knows what she really wants. It's not too late to turn this trend around.

How refreshing would it be for your teenager to know that her mom trusts her enough to be really frank to her about sex, money, love, everything? Her mother lets her know that she doesn't know either, and that this is something to talk over and figure out together. When your children can see your humanity, they will let you see theirs. That's the only way they are going to open up to you later on when they go through rough patches of their lives or when they discover their own sexuality. They reveal themselves to you because you have modeled it to them. But most moms never think of being completely open and honest with their children. Whenever I make this suggestion to my clients, their response is always, "Wow! I can really be that honest with my kids?!" My response is, "Are you kidding me? Don't you want your kids to be honest with you? Yes? Well, then, you should show them what it takes to be honest with them."

Our *priestess* is fiercely protective of the children of the world—actually, she is also fiercely protective of the moms as well. But when it comes down to it, our *priestess* wants all of our children to grow up with access to knowledge about sex, relationships, power, work, leadership, everything. We need to get out of the way and really know how to listen and guide our children. Help them understand what they are experiencing rather than passing down crap that we ourselves are confused about. If we are unsure about something, we should own up to that by prefacing it with something like, "You know, when it comes to this I am really confused myself, so please take whatever I say with a grain of salt." How respectful would that be?

You don't have to figure out sex in order to have a good sex conversation with your kids. You just need to be honest with yourself and with them. Let them embrace you. Let them form their own understanding.

Work

How do the 3Ps™ show up in your business?

When it comes to business, our *peasant* tends to be weak-willed; she has to be a good girl, and so we have to work hard to earn our way up. If you are good enough, the thinking goes, you will be seen and appreciated and eventually promoted. Well, that's only half the equation, and even then it's not always true. Nine out of ten women find themselves working really hard only to be known as a go-to (dumping ground) place. It's like, "Shoot, we have to get this done. Give it to her." And so those piles of work keep getting bigger and bigger. We don't feel like we have the right to say no. We keep saying yes, allowing and training people to treat us badly. Finally, we don't know how to turn that relationship around when it all becomes too much. To cope, we shield ourselves and operate from a place of guilt and fear that we are not good enough and that we haven't done enough. We keep thinking that success is just around the corner, money is just around the corner, the client is just around the corner, if we could just do a little more. We don't know how to receive, how to ask for help, how to surrender to what we don't know. While we should be acting from a place of wisdom, we instead operate from fear, chaos, and a deep sense of unworthiness.

Our *peasant* is scared to death when she goes into a meeting and doesn't have a voice; she is not confident in herself, so when she is asked something, she holds back her true opinion and tries to say things to fit in, to conform to other people's expectations of her. She doesn't let her wisdom out because her truths might rock a few boats, or ruffle feathers. She settles for being mediocre so that she will be liked, then she gets angry because she is not heard. She is angry that nobody sees her, respects her, or promotes her.

Her health suffers. Her salary suffers because she doesn't feel like she can ask for more money. Deep down inside she believes that she is not worth it. She doubts herself, so she bottles up her feelings and her knowings until she either blows up or develops cancer or becomes so resentful and frustrated that she becomes unpleasant to work with. No one wants to be near her, let alone love, adore, and cherish her.

This leaves our *peasants* with no love and very little support—all alone, carrying full responsibility, and still feeling guilty for not having done enough. It's crazy, I know, but it is so true for 99.9 percent of women out there. At worst, some women never question this insanity and beat themselves up about it: *What's wrong with me? Why can't I figure this out? I am _____ years old now, I should have known this by now!*

Asking for help is not a sign that you are not good enough or that you haven't done enough (if you have, indeed, given it your best to this point—we do still need to be responsible for ourselves). It is a sign of humility and curiosity and collaboration. It is a sign that you want to do better and know better, and you care about the success of the business. The *peasant* can't tell people that she doesn't know something because that would be admitting that she is weak and not good enough—but you can.

Eventually, the victim *peasant* will become the angry *peasant*. She will work harder to prove that she is better. *What the !#%#? Those people are not as good as I am and they charge more than I do. What is wrong with this picture?* She is more pissed off, more mistrusting of the world, more isolated and toxic. Clients and opportunities can smell this a mile away and they will avoid her like the plague.

Sadly, this is all happening because she doesn't respect herself. She doesn't trust herself, she doesn't promote herself, she is not even an advocate for herself. This feeling of unworthiness carries over from her work and shows up in her world at large. She doesn't date, or if she does she complains that "he" is not this or that, or she wonders why she meets such unpleasant men. If she has a husband, he may be cheating on her, or their marriage is cold and boring like three-day-old rice.

A lot of women would rather hide behind the story that everything is okay. Maybe things are not great, but they're okay: *I am not happy, but I am okay. Who am I to complain? You know, I am luckier than most people, so I'd better just take my luck and get the best out of it.* This is *peasant* logic. She is used to settling and making do with very little.

It takes *a lot* for a woman to reach her breaking point, to surrender to "Help me!" and to do something about her situation. A *peasant* will push herself to exhaustion until her body breaks down before she lets herself be helped. This is not necessary, and it shouldn't be so. It only depletes us and interferes with our capacity to raise our children and be successful at work. It also pushes love and money away. It's a formula that doesn't work, but we keep repeating it and expecting different results.

We need to help our *peasant* heal. We have to introduce her to an easier way. This is where our *princess* comes in. The *princess* is our champion, and she offers love every step of the way. She says things like, *I am so proud that you woke up early this morning. You deserve tea!* And after you've put yourself together, she says, *You look nice in that outfit, and I am so proud of you. You're going to meet with that potential client and you are very brave. You are lovely; I will be right there with you and we are going to rock this meeting. Because we are awesome and have so much value to offer.* These are not the typical kinds of conversations we have in our heads. We tend to be much more critical of ourselves, and say things like, *Why are you this stupid? Why can't you figure it out?*

Our *peasant* talks trash about herself in the most disrespectful and inhumane ways. Yet we think nothing of it. If you are like my clients, you might be thinking about the *princess* talk above: *That's awkward! I can't say that! It's not natural. That is not true. I don't love myself. I am not proud of myself all the time. I can't say that I look good. I don't feel that.* See what I mean? Your *peasant* will resist your *princess*. Think about it;

how can you expect yourself to go out and do business or date when you are internally shaken like that, when you feel insecure about who you are and your own self-worth?

Let your *princess* and *priestess* lead while your *peasant* follows along to do the practical stuff—clean the office, organize the bills, send out the invoices. Your *princess* comes in first with her grace, gentleness, and generosity. She sets the standard for how people should treat her and she knows what she wants. Your *priestess* follows with her wisdom, clarity, free will, and power. Your *peasant* will feel safe and confident, and she will trust that she knows what she is doing. Easy-peasy!

This is how I work now. When things are hard, I just stop, sit back, and think to myself, 'Things are hard right now. I am just going to breathe, wait, and see what needs to happen next.' I would ask my *princess*, "If I were not afraid, what would I really want right now?" An answer would come to me. Then I would ask my *priestess*, "What is the truth here? What is most important?" Finally, I would ask my *peasant*, "What do I need to do now? What kind of support do I need?" The answer is always clear, the actions are always correct, and the outcomes are always awesome and amazing.

Is there anything else we should say about the 3Ps™ and building your work and business?

Work and business can and should be a lot of fun. It is fun and easy when the 3Ps are working together! You need your *peasant* to do the practical stuff. You need your *princess* to know your birthright and what is true to you. The *princess* also brings in magic. The joy and lightness from the *princess* attracts magic and miracles to us. Then we need our *priestess* to tap into our wisdom and our power. How do we want the world to be? How do we want to be in the world? What is most important for the highest good? Your *priestess* always know. Let her wisdom express itself through your work. Look up powerful and inspirational people; they are that way because they have followed their *priestess* and *princess* guidance to do life their way. Google David Garrett; he is a hot man playing the violin like a *king* and *magician*. Look at Angelina Jolie. I talk about her often in my speaking engagements. She is first a *priestess*, then a *princess,* then a *peasant*, in that order. She is doing powerful work in the world as an actress, a filmmaker, a humanitarian, and a mom of six children. She has been cited as Hollywood's highest-paid actress by Forbes magazine in not one but three different years.

When we are supported and guided from the inside out, with our 3Ps™ powerfully integrated, we rock the world. It's a lot easier to let in life to help us. When we are insecure, we block love, success, and money. We don't let in wisdom, we don't let in other people to help us, and we make everything extremely hard. Our *peasant*s alone will run our careers and businesses into the ground with exhaustion and insecurity.

Dating and your Ex

The ex equation is a humongous piece of a woman's new life. Frankly, you will never be done with your ex if he is the father of your children. The ex factor will anchor a woman who is dating again into her *peasant* self! Things you have to deal with, like the ex behaving badly, make your *peasant* crazy and protective of the children so that you are not free to date. Or consider the internal guilt and shame that your *peasant* puts on you: "Oh my God, I failed in that relationship. How can I do this one?" Remember, your *peasant* loves to feel bad, work harder, and prove that she is good enough, that life is hard and that she will not get what she wants. The ex adds lots of fuel and "support" to the *peasant* woman's struggle with dating again.

When a woman is divorced, she has finally gotten her ex out of her life. Yet when she is dating again or thinking about dating, the ex pops back into her mind. He shows up in the fear that resides in her head. Secretly she is afraid that she will repeat the same patterns again. The bad or good sex that she had with her ex still resides in her body. She might not even know it. Most of the time she doesn't make the connection, but it's there.

She compares every new experience with what happened between her and her ex. The result manifests itself as either her *peasant* clamping her legs tight or splaying her legs wide open, unconsciously.

The ex's influence also shows up in her kids. She looks at the children and sees their father. She remembers his approval or disapproval of her choices. One of my clients shared her revelation. She had been divorced for many years. She was proud of the fact that she was on good terms with her ex. They were friends. She had dated a few men since the divorce, but nothing serious had come of it. One day during one of my classes, she burst out laughing, as she realized that she had brought her ex with her in her mind to all the dates she had been on!

A woman knows that she has to make space for her new love. But she can't because her guilt is so big. Remember, *peasant*s love to feel guilty. She can be dropping off her kids with her ex and be on her way to her boyfriend. It probably takes the whole drive to the boyfriend's to shake off her guilt that she left her kids with someone else, even if that someone is their father!

She hides her new life from her kids because she is ashamed of her desire or her choices. She uses the excuse of, "I don't want the kids to think that every man I am with will be their new father. That will confuse them." But the truth is that she does not approve of her own choices.

Another way women trip up over the ex is how we continue to expect them to treat us with a sense that we still matter to them. I have to admit, I am guilty of this. Even though we are divorced, secretly I still want my ex to have more consideration of my needs, or to show that our "we" (him, me, and my daughter) still matters over other, newer things (like his new girlfriend). HA! It's OVER. Most men no longer give a fuck about the old family they once had. Men think compartmentally, and women think globally. When men are divorced, they are done. They'll get rid of those old feelings, cut all ties with us, and move forward. We are still trying to plan family Christmas dinner with everyone, then our *peasant* gets pissed because they don't give a damn!

It doesn't matter if you've been divorced for one year or for twenty years. There is probably still going to be that sense of old loyalty that sticks to you like stepped-on bubble gum. The *peasant* was trained for so long to be loyal, to shut down everything else to be with this one man forever. Then divorce happened and that forced her to open back up and let new love in. It can be really hard for her to open up and think about dating and creating a new relationship, let alone having sex with a new man.

On the other hand, there are women who are seduced by the "big romance" and the hot sex. Not long after being divorced, especially if what caused the divorce was the fact that the woman fell madly in love with a new man, she thinks, 'Oh my God, this is it. This is the love I've been looking for! I didn't have it with my ex, but I have it now. This is going to be the answer to my everything!"

This kind of reaction seems like redemption, but it isn't always. Sometimes things really are this simple. The romance works out, and they live happily ever after. More often than not, this is what actually happens. In the beginning it's all good. All those endorphins that we call "love" create wonderful, warm, fuzzy feelings and amazing sex. You can't get enough of each other. But after three months, or a year or two, the feelings start to fade. The woman panics and ends up chasing that old "in love" feeling. She will chase that feeling either with this man or the next. The truth is that in the long run you're going to have to undo whatever old patterns you inevitably bring into your new relationship. You have to face healing those patterns in order for the new love to last.

Then there is the hardworking woman who hides behind her kids to avoid the vulnerability of dating again. "I have to take care of my kids." "I have all these things to do." "My kids come first! He will just have to deal with that." What she is secretly saying is, "I don't want to be treated like I was treated by my ex." "I don't want to be hurt, cheated on, or disappointed by a man again." They don't want to be vulnerable, to open up and be dropped again. The painful memories of the ex are still haunting them.

As you can see, when it comes to the ex and dating again, the poor *peasant* has a lot to wrestle with: her guilt, her shame, her old loyalty, her shut-down desire, her insecurity, her heavy load of responsibility, etc. This is why most divorced moms who are dating again find it so challenging to have a fun and successful dating life. They end up hurting themselves instead of finding true love. The *peasant* needs her *princess* and *priestess* to help her with her relationship with the ex.

Her *princess* will gently encourage her to leave her guilt behind, open up to new love and pleasure, trust that she will be safe and attract the kind of men who will help her heal old wounds. She will show the *peasant* what it is like to have men adore you. The *peasant* will reclaim her own worth and beauty.

Her *priestess* will keep her safe, command respect, take ownership of any situation, and give her the freedom to enjoy sex and pleasure however she likes it. Her *priestess* will help the *peasant* grow up around love and relationships. No more gushy, romantic, Disney love stories; instead she will cultivate lasting love from the inside out. She will show the *peasant* what it is like to have men cherish you, which means worshiping you and the ground you walk on, and giving the *peasant* the freedom to be whom she longed to be.

Worksheet #6

You, Your Ex, and Dating

Often women set out to date, not realizing that they have not gotten over their ex. They are still fearful of their disappointment from their ex, or are so engrossed with being friends with their ex that they actually have shut down to other possibilities. Let's do a clearance check shall we?

How present is your ex in your mind, body and heart?

Are you worried about your ex's judgment of your new lifestyle or decisions?

Are you still mad at him for something? (this is a really important question to answer thoroughly.)

Do you find yourself comparing men to your ex?

Do you worry all men are like your ex?

What other ways do you think about your ex in relationship to dating?

How did you do? Is the coast clear? Or do you need to do some clean up work?

Join my online community to help you get rid of this stuff. http://www.hotlifehotlove.com/divorced-moms-dating-guide Like my page and send me a message to add you to my private group.

Mai Vu Coach
www.maivucoach

www.hotlifehotlove.com

Some women deal with psychotic exes who try to control them or who are still trying to get them back. The ex will beg the woman to come back to the relationship. That's very tricky for someone to maneuver through. Again, her *peasant* is going to be triggered into feeling guilty, like she's responsible for his feelings. Her *peasant* will want to rebel, say, "No, I'm done with this," break free, and try to do things from a righteous, rebellious place rather than from a place of, "This is my rightful place. This is where I want to be. This is what I'm creating for myself, and I'm going to be up front and clean about it. If you guys like it or don't like it, I'm here. We can walk through your dislikes and I'm going to keep going." That's really hard to do, and most of us don't have those kinds of models. We have only one model passed down to us, which is to hide everything. Whatever you do is shameful, and you don't want people to judge you. Therefore, hide it and don't talk about it. Hide it from your children and hide it from everybody, and, well, you may have temporary peace in the moment, but in the long run you damage your relationship, you're not communicating with your kids, and you don't trust that others are capable of understanding you.

Then there is the situation where the ex is an alcoholic or has other issues that he's going through. Most likely, if he is going through a lot of issues, and he is not getting help. He is not talking to a coach or counselor. You feel really torn about how to send your kid over to your ex's. This can become such a huge conflict, that many times the woman will opt out of a date or other commitment because she is a good mother and must protect her kids.

Understanding Men

Okay, so we've talked about you, your kids, your work, and your ex. Now, before I send you out into the world of dating, let's talk about men in general. You have your 3Ps™ to guide you, but what about the men? Do they have their version of the 3Ps™ too? Yes, and their archetypes are slightly different. Being aware of this will help you understand and empathize with men better.

Men as Peasants

Just as women have their *peasant* self, men have their *peasant* as well. This is your sensitive, nice guy, the one who comes along to get along. He's reliable and hardworking, and has low to medium self-esteem. He tends to let others have their way and sacrifices his own needs in order to please other people. He is great for co-parenting, as he would happily wear the baby carrier, push the baby carriage, and hold your purse when you go to the restroom. He has a stable job, and would be content working at the same place for the rest of his life to provide for his family. He can be super reliable and self-sufficient. He is an ideal man to most *peasant* women…until it gets super boring because stability and earnestness are all he has access to. He is afraid to be more than that. The *peasant* man can also become angry and irritated, or even be an alcoholic if he is unhappy with his life because he doesn't have the self-awareness or tools to express himself.

Have you ever been with a man and felt utterly bored with your passionless relationship? It's probably because you were both stuck in *peasant* mode and couldn't get out.

Men as Princes

Lots of women want a Prince Charming, but they don't really know what they are getting. Yes, he is handsome, charming, and debonair. Everybody likes him and wants him. He's confident and smooth, and he says all the right things. There are lots of these guys in the personal growth/ spiritual development world. There is even a name for them: "spiritual gigolos." The *prince* tends to avoid hard work, real commitment, and sticking around through the tough times. Deep down, it's all about him! He is lazy and has somehow found a way to get women, from his mom to his dates, to take care of him. A *prince* needs a *peasant* woman to take care of him financially, emotionally, and physically. This is not hopeless, however. When a *prince* gets to be with a *priestess*, she will help him grow into a *king*.

Are you attracted to men whom you end up taking care of? Have you resented a man in the past because you felt like you had to take care of him? If so, you have had a Prince Charming, just like you always dreamt of. Unfortunately, it's not what you were hoping for.

Men as Kings

A man needs to eventually become king of his own kingdom to live a fulfilling life. He tends to get there around forty-five to fifty years old. He has put in his time as a good, reliable *peasant*. With experience, positional power, and wealth, he claims his throne over his own kingdom. He is established and is not afraid to be in charge. He protects and provides for his family and clan. He commands the respect of his community. He has his opinions and his way of doing things. He takes others' needs into consideration, but he ultimately makes his own decisions and lives in his power.

A *king* will help a *peasant* woman rise into her *princess* self with his love and protection. He loves to have a *princess* to take care of. When he is with a woman who enjoys being a *princess*, it makes him younger, stronger, and more powerful. On the other hand, being with a *king* helps a woman feel safer and cared for. It's easier for her to surrender and drop into her softer *princess* self. This is why you see a lot of older men and younger women coupled together. It works well for both sides.

Unfortunately, often a strong *peasant* woman will butt heads with a *king*, trying to dethrone him. This dynamic does not serve either one.

Men as Magicians

Being a *king* alone is not enough. There comes a time when a *king* is called to be more, to dive deeper into his own mystery, his invisible power, to create a legacy or to help cultivate others into *kings* or *priestesses*. Just like Merlin to King Arthur, or Gandalf to the kingdom, a man steps into his own magic to serve a higher cause. He taps into his secret power to change the world. It may be his photography, his "thing" that he has tinkered with in the garage for the last few decades, or that he uses his time and money to support a meaningful cause. As a *magician*, he needs alone time to be creative and tap into his mystery to bring forth his wisdom/art/craft. When a *magician* is invited to serve a cause and he gets to give his all, he feels a sense of purpose, like he's leading a life worth living. He will go as far as giving his life to it, gladly. A *magician* will help a *peasant* woman step into her *priestess* self, or mentor a young *prince* to become a *king*, or partner with a *priestess* and become Twin Flames, having a huge impact on the world.

CHAPTER FIVE

Getting Back Out There

I know this is hard to hear, and perhaps it's even harder to follow, but don't date to find a relationship. Date so that you can find yourself. Teach yourself how to enjoy each moment for what it is, to enjoy each person as is. First, you must learn how to love unconditionally. The *peasant* "loves" so that she can get love, control love, and own love. Let your *princess* and *priestess* show you what love can really be like.

Let go of planning for the future. Let go of deciding whether or not he's the one. This kind of thinking is so detrimental, and it won't get you the results you want. But when you can just start playing with men, flirting with them, letting yourself be taken out by men and not trying to build a whole future out of it, suddenly your future will start to build itself. This path that I am guiding you toward takes a bit of external guidance so that you can help your *peasant* heal and grow. This, in turn, will build confidence, freedom, and joy for you. From this place you will find your man, you will have love that is lasting, hot and powerful. It will pay off, I promise.

So, it sounds like you need to suspend your existing beliefs and just have trust in the process that things are going to work out and that people are going to start showing up in your life because you're going to naturally attract and meet the right kind of people, right?

Yes, and then, because you're in touch with yourself and you now have the skills that I taught you, you can actually maneuver through conversations and situations so much better than you did before. You'll end up with the outcome you want instead of repeating the same old patterns of behavior that left you wanting more.

Okay, now I'm going to give you some tough love. I'm going to ask you, even if you don't believe in this yet, to throw out the usual mindset you would bring to this and approach it this way. This is hard; it's normal to have resistance, and the *peasant* is going to be wounded. It's tough to sort that out, but listen: you aren't going to be doing this by yourself. I don't want your *peasant* resistance and cynicism and woundedness to keep you from moving forward on your path to wholeness. For now, just go with it knowing that these are the tools I use with my clients. Know that you'll have resistance, and it's normal to work through that. It's all a part of the process. Do the best you can with this and put your resistance mind on pause for a moment. Just do the exercises and feel for yourself whether there's a sense of relief, whether you feel better from one particular section or exercise. If you do feel better, trust it. Learn to trust. You'll feel good. That means you're going in the right direction. Don't quit. Don't let that voice that says, "Yeah, but . . ." interfere. If you hear that nagging voice, just pause a minute longer and keep doing the exercises.

Can you give an example of what this new kind of dating looks like?

Dating becomes really fun when you're not attached to the outcome and stressing about the future, because now you're not dating to find "the one." You are dating to find yourself. Dating becomes a series of fun experiments instead of the rigged game where you always lose. Each time you go out with someone, you make it into a scavenger hunt, finding a piece of yourself that you lost a long time ago. For example, when you go out on a date, practice being really honest—kind, but honest. See how it goes. See what you discover. Another date, you practice not doing or saying things to impress him. Or try to be really intimate, but don't have sex. Or practice having really great sex with someone and don't exchange phone numbers. Practice non-attachment.

Up to now, you've likely never been honest with yourself when it comes to dating or otherwise, and so you'll be pretending, and your date will pick up on that so he'll pretend, and then neither of you is having a real conversation. But if you're out there practicing having an honest conversation and letting go of your agenda of impressing this guy, "tricking" him into liking you so that one day he'll marry you, you're on a different track. You're on this track of dating from your heart. You're speaking from your true self, from your body, from your pleasure, and from your present moment.

We've all heard about "being in the moment." How do you do that? You practice it every step of the way, little by little. For example, say you're on a date and you're wondering who's going to pick up the check for dinner. You think, *I want to be taken out. I want to be treated, and I want to just fully receive. When the check comes, I'm not going to offer to pay half of it from a place of unworthiness. I'd like for him to pay. Maybe down the line I'll choose the restaurant and I can treat him.* Okay, great. So practice asking for that. Before you go out, you might say something like this to him: "So…I am practicing receiving and not feeling obligated to pay back. Would you enjoy taking me out and treating me like a *princess*? Would you like to be the hero? If you are good with that, we'll have a fun game. If that bothers you, we won't."

I'd like to share with you the story of a woman who has been chatting online with this guy. She keeps wondering why he hasn't asked her out yet, and then he starts to text less and the texts become more impersonal. At first, their messages were hot and heavy and he seemed really curious about meeting her, but now he'll respond only if she texts him. First of all, that in itself is a sign that he has lost interest or has moved on to pursuing another woman. My suggestion would be to let this guy go completely. Don't wait around and pine for him. If a man shows the slightest sign of not being interested, you're done and out. Cut it clean. Don't make excuses for him.

Another way to handle it, I suggested to her, is to be really upfront. Just say, "I would love to meet you in person and be taken to dinner by you next weekend. Would you want to do that?" If he says no, now you know, and it's done. If he says yes, he has a clear direction. He knows what you want, and he's saying that he can provide that. You could even say, "Here's where I'd like to go," or "Here's what I'd like to do."

Let's recap. Redefine the purpose of dating. Stop calling it "dating." Call it "catch and release program," or "doing a series of experimentations," or "doing a PhD for yourself on dating." For yourself, right? Because when people date to find a partner for life, it's too serious. You show up and you're so serious, and you've got your long list of requirements and expectations and previous wounds and hurts, and you want to make sure he doesn't do any of that, and . . . When this happens, you're not even seeing that person for who he really is. It does not serve you or the man. But if you approach this as an experiment, that changes everything. You are free to have fun and play.

I think dating, work, and everything, really, come from a place of knowing who you are and knowing that you are free to create. If you want to know who you are, look at the people who show up around you. What are they mirroring? If you encounter men who are angry and skeptical, ask yourself, "Where am I angry and skeptical?" Heal that and those men will stop coming around. If you complain that the men you meet are not available to you, look inside. Where are you not available to life?

Furthermore, when you can articulate clearly what you're working on, the men will be right there, responsive to your desire. Everything starts with learning how to communicate what you want and need. Most women make it about the men. Men don't do this or that. But really, if you ask them what they want, the answer is usually, "I don't know." The first and perhaps most important lesson in getting back out there is that you need to learn to be able to speak what you want, to trust that what you want is valid and that there will be lots of people who will want to provide that for you.

*It seems like a lot of people would actually be really relieved to hear
someone just spell out what they want?*

Yes, they are. Very. I've never had a woman come back to me and
say, "Mai, that did not work. I told him what I wanted and the date went
sideways." Usually the reverse is true. "Mai, my date didn't work," and
when I ask them, "Did you tell him what you wanted up front?" their
answer is, "No, I can't say things like that up front." And then, "I can't
even imagine saying that," or they go out of their way to please the other
guy. Then the date doesn't go well and they're disappointed.

But what if you were to casually say, "Hey, can I tell you something
honest about myself? I'm looking at this whole dating thing, and it scares
me to death. I'm not good at it, and right now what I want to work on is
just being really honest with my communication. Are you good with that?"
The guy's probably going to say okay. That probably scares him a little,
but that's all right. He's up for it. Men love challenges. He will most likely
say, "Oh, yeah, tell me more."

That's when you say, "Okay, for this date, I would love to go out
with you and I want to go to..." You could even name what you want to
experience. Oh my gosh, men love that. You might even hear them say
spontaneously, "Yes, *princess*, how can I serve you?"

Let's consider where love, relationship, and sex come into play

Let me pause for a second.. I wanted to pull apart these three areas
in order to understand each one better. I bet there was a time in your life
when you thought you knew everything about yourself. But then, after a
separation, a divorce, and life after the divorce, maybe you realized that
you didn't know everything there was to know about yourself. That's okay.
This is a tremendous learning experience (albeit a painful one), but you're
going to come out on the other side knowing yourself a whole lot better.

Divorce and dating again is your chance to really experience what
love means. How do you express love? How do you receive love? What

does it take for you to feel love from someone? These are deep questions that you may not have thought about recently, if ever. But dating again will allow you to find out.

This is also the time in your life when you get to experience sex. What you know about sex and relationship you learned from high school. You are older and wiser; it's time for you to develop a much deeper relationship to your sex. Can you have wholesome sex for the sake of sex and pleasure and not tie it to a relationship? Why is this so important? Simply put, because your sex belongs solely to you. It is your job to learn to have great sex despite your partner. We are so codependent when it comes to sex. I hear this all the time. "Oh, I can only have sex if I am emotionally connected to him." "He was sooooooo good." "Now that he is gone, no one else measures up." These are the thoughts that cause us suffering and misery. They make us dependent on another being and we miss ourselves.

What I discovered after my personal PhD program of sampling thirty-three men in three years blew me away. At the end of my experiment, I was able to have multiple-orgasms and amazing sex with just about anyone. I went from rigid "I can't come vaginally" to coming twenty-plus times in one night, as long as a man could last. AND what's most important was that I did not need his phone number afterward to make me complete. That was when I knew that I was ready for a real and intimate relationship with one man. When I could be intimate with any man.

What does a relationship really mean? Who are you when you're in a relationship with someone? What does it take for you to commit and to be in a relationship, and what do you want out of a relationship? How do you stay safe in a relationship? How do you maintain who you are and not lose your identity in the relationship?

These are really important questions that we rarely ask ourselves. We blindly seek The One so that we can fall madly in love and live happily ever after. I don't know how many divorces you need to go through to know that this is not how it works. That this business of falling madly in love and living happily ever after exists only in a Disney film. Even in those fairy tales, Disney is rewriting them one by one to tell the real story behind the facade. Love and relationship are not a boring, one-dimensional tale of simply living happily ever after. They're much more complex and rich. Unpacking our answers to all these questions about love, sex, and relationship is critical.

How does dating differ if you are recently divorced versus having been divorced a while?

Someone who is recently divorced is freshly wounded. Maybe she was dumped by her husband. In this case, she is completely devastated, completely blindsided. The person she thought was her rock, her man, is gone. So she doubts herself. Now she has proof that she's not good enough to be with a man because if she was, he never would have left her.

If she tries dating, she's like a skittish cat. If she's lucky, she'll meet a man who wants to love her, but she can't trust it and will do everything she can to push him away. She will find a reason to cancel dates at the last minute. She'll hide behind her kids. Deep down, she's way too vulnerable to open herself up again.

But the thought of being lonely and alone, and the shame of that, is so much. Her girlfriends and her family give her terrible advice: "You should date. You should get back on the horse and date again right away." Heck no! That is the *last* thing you want to do if you are still feeling wounded. You need to sit still. You need to heal yourself. You need to weep and get to know who you are because you have likely lost yourself in the last five, ten, fifteen years of marriage. You probably don't know who you are without this man. Rediscovery is paramount, and that's what we've been working on through this whole book.

Who is this woman who has been gone, who's lived through this betrayal? What does this woman want? What does this woman like? I think this woman probably has a lot of new ideas in her head, in her heart, with which she needs to reacquaint herself. And she's usually overwhelmed with obligations and pressure at the same time. Marriage is this cocoon, this safety net. Maybe there are financial hardships as a result of the divorce. Money strain is a very real pressure and is not to be overlooked or minimized. Right after a divorce, there's a lot of scrambling going on. Scrambling to get a better job, perhaps. Scrambling to figure out what went wrong in the marriage. Scrambling to arrange what to do with the kids, where they will go, and how they're doing emotionally.

Therefore, right after a divorce is not the time to date. It's a time to let people come in to help, to let people come in to share their love. Don't feel compromised or obligated to return the love, either. This is one of the few times in life when you get to say, "I don't have anything to give you back right now. I am a mess. I don't trust anything. I don't trust anybody. So I appreciate your being here with me and wanting to love me and I'm going to let you love me, but please don't expect anything in return." How refreshing is that, to be able to be honest. That's the freshly divorced woman.

For the woman who's been divorced a while…she is rusty. It's like the job market—the longer you stay out of dating or the job market, the harder it is to get back in. Yes, after a divorce you need time to heal and regroup. One to three years is enough. Any more than that, you are hiding. It really is important for you to let love back in, to let someone love, adore, and cherish you. You will be safe, I promise.

How long should we wait to date again? How will we know when we're ready?

Well, the short answer is that you'll know when it feels right. That's really true for all women. You know when you're ready if you're in touch with yourself. That's why doing all the work in this book up to this point is so important.

Unfortunately, most women don't know how to heal themselves and guide themselves forward. They are much more in touch with second-guessing and beating themselves up. Maybe they are addicted to having a man or are just hiding. They're much more in touch with their judgment than with who they are and what they want. In this case, it's time to seek professional help. But what kind of professional help? Here is what I discovered after twenty years of doing this. In order to heal and start dating again, an individual needs layers of support. She needs the one-on-one to address the issues that are unique to her. But doing that alone, she will move at a very slow pace. She also needs a community of other women who are going through a similar situation, so that she can see herself in others. When she does, she will realize that she is not alone, that her resistance and fears are not real, and that the group energy will allow the individual to propel forward faster. When I work with clients, they have layers of support so that they can make the changes in three or six months.

Other things that can help are: taking meditation classes; taking other kinds of classes (professional ones or just for fun); and going to counseling. You can do all of it. There are so many forms of support out there to help you connect to who you are and be successful in moving forward. Taking advantage of these opportunities not only helps you directly, it also helps you build new relationships and it helps keep your mind from spiraling into the negative place it probably wants to go after such a traumatic event.

Take three to six months to heal yourself and to really look at these patterns. Is all this work pointing to a place where you feel really empowered and thriving if you are dating? If you feel like you are getting younger and more beautiful, keep going.

Know that whatever you're doing, wherever you are, it's fine. If you feel scared or stressed about men, these are indications that you need more time and guidance to heal. I promise you this, once you are truly ready for love and truly ready for a relationship, it will show up right in front of you in the most magical way. You do not need to spend so much time online dating or kissing frogs like your friends tell you to do. Once you start to stabilize your *peasant* and help her feel loved, appreciated, and safe, and she gets to know her *princess*, you will have men begging for your attention.

What about the woman who's been divorced for ten, fifteen, even twenty years? How will she know if she's ready to date again?

If you have the inclination, even just once in awhile, that it would be nice to have a man in your life again, that's a good sign that you're ready to date. And this situation is actually kind of awesome because you don't have the financial constraints anymore, and your kids have grown up. You have the time and space. You can actually bring someone into your home and you don't have to worry about privacy or trying to figure out where your children are. You still have to do all the same inner work, but the logistics are much easier to coordinate.

Where this may be trickier is that the layers of resistance to dating are much stronger than they are for the freshly divorced woman. The years that you have been without a man have given you plenty of time to come up with lots of excuses for not wanting a man at all.

First things first, let's call out all of your resistance mechanisms. I would say that eighty-five to ninety percent of all your strategies for your daily life are actually resistance cleverly disguising itself. Thoughts like, 'I have to work,' 'I don't have time and space for a man today,' 'I'm too old,' or 'I don't want to lose my freedom' are all excuses.

The more stable you are by yourself, the thicker your layers of resistance and the riskier dating seems. We need to help your *peasant* understand that she's actually going to be safe and in much better shape if she learns to let love back in. When she learns to receive, her life will be so much easier and more fun. Her heart will be so much lighter and her smile will be so much bigger.

We also need to create a vision. This is surprisingly difficult for women who have sat still for a while. They actually don't have a vision of a man whom they would like to be with. They have a clear vision of what they *don't* want: a man with kids; a man who's sick; a married man, or one who has lots of baggage, or is unstable. They have lots of scary zombie visions about the man they would be stuck with, but if I ask them to draw up a picture of the man they *do* want to be with, it takes them days to do that, sometimes months. One of my clients took nine months to make her vision board of the man she wanted to date.

How does this impact their dating?

Divorced moms who are dating again usually feel some level of guilt. They think of dating through the filter of what they went through with their ex. Emotionally, they're not complete and clean and clear. So that's one entanglement.

If it's a fresh divorce, they still feel guilty about the prospect of sharing a bed with a new guy, especially if they're currently working through the divorce and it's kind of sticky. They have to hide their new love from the ex. They can't be honest because they think the ex is going to use that against them in the divorce decree, and then they try to protect the children from them dating because they have so much shame and guilt surrounding the fact that they're having great sex with this new man. Even just dropping the kids off at the ex's can be very tricky emotionally.

CHAPTER SIX

Dating with the 3Ps™

Let's talk about how to date.

C urrently, people date like a *peasant*, and because the *peasant* is limited in her thinking, she doesn't think she's worthy; she doesn't think that she deserves a lot of anything. She's afraid and just wants safety and security. She dates from a place of very low self-esteem. She pines for a man. She doesn't think that the man she wants exists, and she withholds sex and love because she's not trusting. She has a lot of baggage and wounds from the past, and then she goes into the dating scene thinking that one man is going to complete her. She's completely seduced by the whole idea of the handsome prince on a white horse coming to whisk her away, and she doesn't want to do any understanding of herself, take any responsibility. She doesn't know what she wants, and she's incapable of being honored with what she wants. She's very confused.

She draws in a man who's also confused or who wants something from her. When he is clear, and no matter what he offers, she either makes it wrong or is unapproachable and not able to get it. She's stuck and she's insecure, and whatever happens, she sits there and overanalyzes the guy. When a man shows signs of not treating her well, she compromises herself instead of seeing it as is, "Hey, he's not interested in me. He's not respecting me. He's not available to me."

Dating is really simple. Is he into you? Is he respecting you? And is he available emotionally, financially, physically? If the answer to all these questions is "yes," then go forward. If there is a "no" in there, then stop. Move on.

There are so many men out there, but many women don't see it that way. In the *peasant* mode, everything is hard; everything is scarce, so she doesn't believe that she can have what she wants. Dating is super tricky, super confusing, super limiting, and the success rate is low. But if you date like a *princess*, things are very different. It's wonderful.

Worksheet #7

Dating Vision Worksheet

Write out your ideal man/men:

What does your *peasant* want in a man?

What does your *princess* want in a man?

What does your *priestess* want in a man? (good question huh? I bet you have never asked yourself this question before)

Mai Vu Coach
www.maivucoach

www.hotlifehotlove.com

When a woman dates from the *peasant*, the *princess*, and the *priestess* together, it's super-hot. Here's what it might look like. If you have your *princess*, if you know you're worthy, you're beautiful, and you deserve to be loved, it's easy-peasy. You don't have to sit there and wonder if a guy's going to reject you. You never have to beg a man for attention. You just show up. You radiate your love, joy, beauty, and confidence. The *princess* is going to attract men like crazy—good men, not lousy ones, because her vibration is so high that like attracts like. The men who come have things to give, they want to serve the Princess, and they're intrigued by this deep mystery behind you. You're not just a pretty face whom men bring home and turn into a trophy wife; you're this beautiful essence who has strength and power behind you, who deserves respect and something more. What is that? That is the essence of being loved, adored, and cherished.

The first couple of rounds, sex is just lovely because he's there serving you and making you feel safe and pleasing your body. Your *princess* is satiated and you feel completely safe. Then the *priestess* comes out and flips him over and rides him until she's satisfied. Who wouldn't like that? Who wouldn't want that? That's in the bedroom, but the same dynamic goes on in life. He takes great care of you. He loves you. He treats you like a *princess*. He's always responsive and there for you. And, in turn, you rock his world.

There are moments in daily life when the *priestess* speaks: *This is where we're going. This is what we need to do.* The man bows to her and says, "Of course. I'm listening. Not only am I adoring you, I'm also serving you and I'm cherishing you." This is very powerful. To be cherished is to be respected and worshiped. Most women run when they hear the word *cherish*. What does that mean, to have a man worship you? What do you have that is worth worshiping? What does it take to stand in a place of knowing that you are worth being worshiped—that it's not an ego game, but is rightfully so? It's your purpose, your calling. You are much bigger than your *peasant* roles. You are here on this planet, at this time in history, for a purpose. He sees that purpose and he wants to worship and support you in bringing it into the world. This gives him meaning, love, and security.

If you have your *princess* and you know you're worthy of being adored, that makes dating so easy. But that alone is not enough because we're up to something in the world. We need a man to also:

1. See our vision,

2. Respect that vision and worship it, and

3. Help us bring that vision into the world.

Your man must do all three of these things. When he sees you in your *peasant* mode, he knows that it's time to help you step into your *princess* so that you can soften and surrender. He must ask himself, *What can I do to protect and cherish her so that she will remember her beauty, her gentleness, and what she's made of?* If he does this, you can surrender out of your hard working *peasant* mode right into your joyful, happy, well-cared-for *princess* mode. He's also always listening. *Okay, my woman is up to something. She's doing her work right now. Let me worship that. Let me listen to her calling. Let me see how I can help bring this calling into the world.* That's responding to the *priestess*, helping her execute her vision.

Wow. Everything is super easy and hot. Hot life, hot love, and hot business, that's what I am talking about. So often nowadays single working mothers are doing it all, and the *peasant* gets exhausted. She needs help. She needs someone to cook for her, rub her feet, support her endeavors with materials and time or whatever it takes to achieve her goal. She can't do it by herself. She needs a loving and devoted partner. She knows her worth so much that she is totally okay with knowing that she deserves a man and a community to support her.

We can't create a partner who will help if we never know that we're entitled to this level of care, that our mission is worth supporting, and that our being is worth loving. I think this is what's most important about the 3Ps™ concept that I am blessed to have channeled through me. The time of us women putting ourselves last, trying to take care of everyone else first, hoping that if we work harder we will achieve what we are called to do is over. We cannot do what we want to do, like help change the world, raise healthy children, and build successful businesses, if we are not loved, adored, and cherished first and foremost. Having our 3Ps integrated and healthy will allow us to accomplish what we are here to do.

How do the 3Ps™ affect a woman's sexuality?

Peasant Sex

We have to start by understanding where a typical woman is. When it comes to sexuality, generally speaking, a woman is very much entrenched in the *peasant* mode, which means, *sex is scary, sex is shameful, sex belongs to someone else, somewhere else, and it should not be pleasurable. If you do enjoy it, you are a slut or a whore. You should hide your sexuality and be a proper woman, a responsible woman.*

When a *peasant* has sex, most of the time she does it because she feels dutiful and responsible. She feels like it is tit for tat, and she has to return the favor. She feels unworthy to receive it, and she feels obligated and encumbered by sex.

We are told the terrible lie that being a good woman can get us where we want, and then we get pissed off when the reality is far from that. Men choose women who are not what we call "good" women all the time, and a good woman doesn't understand why she ends up alone. She has done everything she can to make herself worthy of love. Why can't she get the love, support, and respect she wants?

We are trained to think "good" people do not have certain kinds of sex. Only conventional sex is accepted. But conventional sex—like sex behind closed doors, four-position sex, and quiet sex—is so boring! At some point you need to start exploring sex, reclaiming it, and having more power over it.

I took back my own sexuality when I stopped tying sex to relationships. I believe that you are missing out if you have sex only while you're in a serious relationship. You are not having sex for the pleasure of sex anymore; you are having sex so that you can manipulate, earn, keep, or gain love. That is not pure sex. That is not sex in the body; that is sex in the head. It's using sex to control a situation, to satisfy a need to belong. It is coming from a place of insecurity instead of really celebrating what sex is supposed to be for us.

Princess Sex

From the *princess* perspective, a woman who has her sex is all about understanding pleasure. What does it mean to receive pleasure? What does it mean to give pleasure, not out of a sense of duty or responsibility, but purely for personal satisfaction and enjoyment?

When you are in the *princess* realm, the sex is amazing. Sex is about you. What makes you light up, come alive, scream, get wet? All of that belongs to you, and rightfully so. When you bring in a partner, he or she knows to help elevate you, to help bring you into your full softness, your surrendered, peaceful self. Imagine being able to receive sex without any of the cumbersome stuff that the *peasant* comes to sex with. Imagine applying this to your whole life, knowing that everything that happens has to be for your pleasure. If it's not for your pleasure, it's not right yet.

If it doesn't feel good, it's not right. If it doesn't elevate you and help you radiate and become more, it's not good enough. This is what good sex can teach us. We need to let ourselves have that in the bedroom, in the kitchen, in the living room, in the boardroom, everywhere. If things are not right, you need to stop and acknowledge that you are not satisfied. Your standard has not been met, and the highest good has not been achieved. Don't move forward until your standard is met.

Imagine that! When a woman can surrender and let herself have sex this way, she will realize that she is safe, she can trust herself, and she can trust men to service her, to love her, to adore her, to kiss every inch of her body from the tip of her toes to the top of her head. She can receive it and she doesn't have to feel obligated to return it. If she does, it's because it makes her feel good to do so. That's what I want for myself and for all of us. I want us to learn to live from this place that feels good, to our highest standard so that we walk through life knowing that we are loved, adored, and cherished. We do the same for people around us; we love, adore, and cherish other people. Anyone who comes into our lives feels that energy because we are truly living and embodying it. That is super-hot!

Priestess Sex

Priestess sex is bold, powerful, and expansive. After you are satiated with *princess* sex, your body will naturally stretch into *priestess* sex. This is where you TAKE instead of receive. You are so filled up that something deep and fierce takes over, and she rises up to consume her prey, her man. This may sound scary, but at this level of intensity, her prey is the luckiest being on the whole planet in that moment. Rapture, passion, and chandeliers falling from the ceiling happen here. I have to admit, trying to explain Priestess sex to someone who has never experienced it is like explaining sushi to someone who has never tried it. The more I explain how good raw, cold fish is, the worse it sounds, right? Exploring *priestess* sex is like fathoming the size of the universe; it's limitless. When we have sex this way, we actually help our man step into his power by surrendering to us. I know that sounds contradictory, but it is true. When we allow ourselves to be powerful in the bedroom, we allow our man to have a strong force to which he can surrender. This opens them to a deeper level of vulnerability that they don't normally get to have anywhere else in life. From this vulnerable place, our man reconnects to his real self, his real desire, and his real truth. The man who gets to receive our power in *priestess* sex will finally find a place where he can trust women again. This disconnection from women is the source of deep anger and resentment that most men don't even know they have. But it is there. When we can connect to a man at this level, he will feel safe again and, thus, reclaim his true power. Only a handful of women around the world know this, and it's an amazing, amazing world.

For us women, once we can let ourselves have this level of sex, our minds will open to what is truly possible for ourselves (because we will have met our own power), for humanity, and for relationship because we will be having sex to serve our partner in the most expansive and free form possible.

And it is okay if this paragraph doesn't make any sense to you. It will one day.

How can cultivating the 3Ps™ help us reclaim our sexuality?

This is a very slow and gentle process, and it cannot be rushed. Just like good sex, it's slow and gentle, and then it builds up. If you find yourself rushing toward reclaiming your sexuality or pushing yourself into it, that's your *peasant* trying to accomplish, fix, or prove something. Your *peasant* needs to slow down, feel safe, and gently move forward to create sustainable and healthy change.

It starts with reading the *peasant* mindset—where she is and what is in her mind—to help her see all her fear, resistance, and mistrust of her pleasure. She's been taught to trust pain and hard work. If you bring anything to a woman and say, "To accomplish this, you have to work really hard, and you have to plan to suffer a little bit or a lot, but we promise that if you work really, really hard and stick with it, you are going to get to the end," nine times out of ten the *peasant* will say, "Sign me up. I will learn how to do that."

If you bring sex to a *peasant* and say, "This is actually really yummy. It's amazing, and when you let yourself have this, you will feel amazing joy. Your heart will open wide and you will experience pleasure from head to toe," you know what she will say? "No thanks, that's not for me," or "I don't trust you. That doesn't exist."

We have to meet the *peasant* where she is. We need to love and accept her as is and show what being loved and accepted look like. This gives her the first taste of pleasure. She thinks, 'Oh, really? You would accept me as is and not try to change me? That's new!' Now she can breathe a little deeper and relax a bit.

Helping a *peasant* heal her sexuality is like giving birth. She needs time to dilate and open up. With each round of dilation, she is to endure a wave of discomfort as she undoes a lifetime of pain and bad conditioning. Be careful not to lay it on too thick at first, because she will run if you give her too much love too soon. Peasants don't realize how much they resist love, pleasure, money, and success. We have to gently show the *peasant* that her patterns of thinking are actually resistance; they are not honest and good like she thinks they are.

Now that really blows the *peasant's* mind. The *peasant* realizes that her entire worldview has been built on that belief. Yeah! When you first trust pleasure, you realize that everything that is not in support of that is an excuse. It all starts with this core belief that things have to be hard, and that you have to work really hard to achieve anything worthwhile. Instead, consider that receiving the most pleasure can and does get you what you want.

This is what being guided by the *princess* means. That is what having experienced, amazing sex looks like. Once you understand that wanting pleasure is a *good* thing, you are able to relax and let go of what goes on in your brain. You know that long checklist that's been in the back of your mind all day? When you have sex, it disrupts everything and the checklist goes away. Then you're able to take those feelings of trust, joy, and pleasure back into your life, into your career, into parenting your children, everything. It's okay to feel good! It's actually really good to feel good, and we all need to learn to believe that.

How can reclaiming your sexuality help you reclaim your relationship?

Our sexuality is a power center, just like our brain and our heart. Our brain is the power center to understand, rationalize, create, manifest, and imagine. This is the power center of the *peasant*. Our heart is our capacity to love. Our *princess* occupies the heart center. Sex is an equal power center. This is where the *priestess* resides. When you claim that strength and start to have a relationship to it, you are powerful. And when you are in touch with your power, you are in touch with your full self.

I fly a lot to speak to different audiences. On the plane they always say to buckle your seat belt until the plane stabilizes; then you are free to roam around the cabin. When you reclaim your sexuality, you are free to roam around the world and with other people because you are no longer afraid. There are only two places humans can come from—fear or love. If you are no longer afraid, you are only love!

The reason we don't like people, we pull away from people, we don't trust people, we cannot connect deeply with people, is that we are afraid of our own sexuality. We don't trust that power center below the belly button that belongs to us. If we don't trust that, and if we don't have a relationship to our power center, how can we possibly trust others and have relationships them in that intimate way?

I remember that before my sexual reclamation I was so limited in my knowledge of my sexuality. I was so limited in my knowledge of men. When I had meetings with men, I was scared to death (but didn't know it) because there was a whole mystery sitting across from me that I knew nothing about. Once I learned about my body and had full ownership of my sex, *I began to understand men and how to work with men.* Men became super easy to understand and work with.

Exploring my sexuality taught me that men are actually really cool. For the most part they just want to love, adore, and cherish women. They actually want to give to us, and we unknowingly make it really hard for them to do so. I discovered something very interesting: When I don't allow a man to give and pleasure me, that is when they start to take from me because they don't know what else to do.

If you think about it, a relationship with another person is quite simple: I give to you, you receive. We are happy. You give to me, I receive. We are happy. But if no one is giving or receiving, the only other option is to take from each other, and nobody is happy. The lesson here is "let men give to you, and be good at receiving. Everyone will be happy."

When you are in touch with your sexuality, you are not afraid of your sex; you are open, confident, and bouncing down the street oozing love, sex, and freedom. Wow! That's what an attractive woman is; she is beautiful, she is attractive. Men and women want to be near her because it feels good. Dating becomes really easy. You don't even have to gaze. I see all these people do online dating and they waste all this time with drama when the answer is in their own bodies.

I know, your *peasant* might be triggered here with "but that's not safe!" and "I don't want to attract unwanted attention." That would be your *peasant's* reaction to what I am suggesting. What do your *princess* and *priestess* have to say about the idea of you bouncing down the street full of life and sex? My guess is that they would approve wholeheartedly.

CHAPTER SEVEN

Finding Support on Your Path

What if, as we're practicing these ideas, we need some support? Is there a place where readers can go to find a community of other women who are going through the same things?

I encourage you to contact me on Facebook and then join my private Facebook group, Divorced Moms Who Are Dating Again http://www.hotlifehotlove.com/divorced-moms-dating-guide . Readers can post their success stories and questions there. It is essential for women who are done with going it alone.

Great! Is there a next step, or is it just that you're practicing dating and then you start to see shifts?

Have you heard of the sailing analogy? When you are sailing, if your compass is one degree off, you can end up on a different continent.

As you probably know by now, there are lots of layers to heal and lots to navigate through. New things will continue to surface as you resolve old issues and recognize new ones. Being in a community with other women and being guided by someone who has been there and done that and who knows how to guide you will help you reach your desired destination much faster and with less pain. Every woman will hit something so deep that she can't resolve it herself, such as old family issues or trauma or grief that hasn't been fully dealt with. Rarely can you resolve these kinds of problems yourself.

Doing the exercises in this book can help, too. But you have to really do them. It's not enough to just read through them, think about your answers in passing, and then move on. You need to physically put the book down and start writing. The more you give to these exercises, the more you will get out of them.

So . . . getting to the "hot life, hot love" stuff. Does it just happen?

It actually does. It starts popping up in all different places, and before long you'll start to see what success looks like for you. You'll find yourself smiling more and giggling more. This is a sign that things are happening for you. You'll start to notice that life is just easier overall, in all your endeavors. And you'll start to attract men without having to try.

Let me tell you a story about my client Britta. She is a successful businesswoman who has been divorced for many years. She has life handled, but she wanted more, so she hired me to help her. In less than three months, her heart was healed and opened. This happened to her one fine afternoon in Stockholm.

"I walk along the street and on my way home, I hear my name called out.

I turn around and see an old lover.

Thirty years ago, before my long marriage, I was deeply in love with this man

but we could not make it then.

'I think a lot about you,' he says.

'You are so wonderful. I so much would like to kiss you in this moment, here, now.'

And then we kiss...in the middle of the street...in the afternoon... people moving all around us.

'Take care,' he says.

And I walk back home. I think everyone should kiss more. Me too."

Britta Sjöström

Since then, she has opened up so much that men are coming in to adore her. She recently went to Spain at the invitation of an old friend who just wanted to love and support her as she wrote her second book. So she did. He took care of her in every way she desired. When she came home, the Swedish authority contacted her and informed her that her first book was fabulous, and that they would be turning it into an audio book and putting it in all the libraries in the country. She would not have to do anything. Just enjoy her success.

That's HOT, right? She is not alone in accomplishing this level of success, joy, and pleasure. Every single client of mine has their own amazing stories.

Here is another sweet story:

Another client came to me for advice about dating someone who was interested in her. She was unsure whether she wanted to pursue anything with him. I said, "Well, first, don't date him. Just go out and have fun and play."

"Well, should I tell him that I'm not ready to have sex and all that stuff because I'm still wounded and worried that he'll trigger my feelings wrapped up with my ex?" she asked.

"Absolutely," I said. "Tell him that."

"Really? Isn't that too early?" she pressed.

"No, it's not. Just tell him."

And so she did. She said, "Look, I like going out with you, but I'm not ready to have sex yet. I know you've been, you know, hinting that we should spend the night together, but I'm not ready. I need to really focus. I'm still working through my ex, and that still hurts me."

Her guy responded with, "Yeah, sure. We've got plenty of time to go slow. And who doesn't have baggage?"

This opened up the conversation quite a bit, and guess what? Not long after that, they were having sex. My client reported back that it's been great and it's been intense. She also shared with me that they have talked about things that she and her ex never talked about in the two years they were together. That's a whole new level of connection. You know she is having peace inside. She's feeling joy. She doesn't think about her ex anymore, and she's taking one day at a time—some days gently and slowly and other days quickly. It's whatever she wants to do.

This next story is a little more involved. There was a woman at one of my events who sat and cried the entire two days. She didn't say much. She just cried and cried and cried. Finally, at the end, she said, "I get it. I get it now. I deserve so much better. I am going to learn to let love in. I'm done with my life the way it is. I'm going to turn this around." I was happy for her, but I didn't expect to see her again.

The next day, this woman was driving to work and a car was following her really closely. She drove a little faster. He sped up too. She changed lanes. He followed her. *What is going on with this asshole?* she thought. Finally, he honks at her and she's like, *What?!* He waves for her to pull over. She felt like maybe something was wrong with her car and she was unsafe, so she pulled over. The man jumped out of his car, walked up to her, and gave her his business card. He said, "I've been noticing you and you look so beautiful. I just wanted you to know that. If you're available, I'd like to invite you out." Okay, this is pretty weird and borderline creepy. But listen to what happens next.

At that time in her life, this woman was in a dead marriage. She had a teenage daughter who was disrespecting her, and she was hurting inside. She had gone to my workshop, sat there for two days, and cried and cried.

She had gotten in touch with her *peasant* pain, and finally decided that she was done. The next day that incident happened. She took that interaction as a sign that God wanted more for her. She took the man's card, and that night she went home and told her husband that she wanted a divorce.

Three months later, she had moved out and they'd sold the house. Her husband lived in a flat. She lived with her daughter. Her husband started therapy, cleaned up his act, and begged to be let back into her life. She said she didn't want to get back together, but he could stick around. Not long after that, they started dating, and six months later they fell madly back in love. They continue to live separately so that they can keep doing their own personal work, but he has been so good to her since their split. He apologized for falling asleep on her, for being so resistant, and he became the rock in her life. A few months later, she faced some serious health issues. He stepped up, took care of her, and loved her while she recovered. Now that's hot love. When I say HotLifeHotLove™ I don't mean pretty, fluffy stuff. I mean love in the deep, rigorous way that humans learn to love each other, communicate, stand up for themselves and for each other. It is a lasting love, and it's hot.

LAST WORDS... (FOR NOW)

A lasting relationship with someone requires satisfaction of all 3Ps™. Your *peasant* is looking for a mate, a partner who will share in the chores and responsibilities, getting things done and accomplishing things. Your *princess* wants lusciousness, intimacy, gentleness, adoration, and love. The sex has to be exquisite, delightful, and intimate. Both the *peasant* and the *princess* want to be safe, secure, and cared for. That alone does not make for a healthy long-term relationship because you would be giving up too much. Your *priestess* wants to have freedom to express herself and live out what she is here to do. She must have freedom to create, change, commune with the world in a way that will bring out all of YOU. This often creates tremendous fears in your *peasant*. Your *princess* understands your *priestess,* so she is fine, but your *peasant* will often feel like your *priestess* is wrecking everything she has worked so hard to build.

When two people come together and do not understand this invisible yet demanding dynamic, over time the struggle for understanding begins. That struggle, if not understood, becomes a fight for domination: I am right, you are not. My needs are more important than your needs. The truth is that both partners need this. He longs to feel his own *king* inside, to be powerful and command his world. He doesn't just want to be a nice guy who pleases his partner and pleases everyone else around him. He longs for connection to a much bigger mystery and power in him, his own *magician* or *wizard*. The male partner also struggles with finding his 3Ps™ and integrating them so that he can be all that he can be.

If you both know that this is the dynamic at play, you can empower it. When you are in your *peasant*, he can respond to you as a *king* and make you feel safer and cared for—if you empower him, if you don't fight him and judge him wrongly for being a "dick." He is just trying to assert his power so that you can surrender to your *princess*. When you drop into your *princess,* it will allow him to embody his *king* more fully. That alone is not enough. Being a *king* all the time is tiring for any man. He also needs a place to surrender to. That's when you step up into your *priestess*; your power, magnificence, and vision create a container for him to happily serve. He doesn't need to lead and be in charge, He can be his good *peasant* who just wants to serve his *priestess*. The reverse is true, too. Your *princess* inspires him to step into his *king*. From there he naturally will reach for his *magician*. *What else is here for me to do? What is my real purpose? magician* place. When he does that, you can naturally fall into your *peasant* self and serve his cause, which makes him even more powerful. This fluid dynamic that we maintain for each other keeps the relationship HOT for a lifetime!

ABOUT THE AUTHOR

The first certified Asian female CoActive coach in the world, Mai Vu came onto the budding coaching scene twenty years ago, fell in love with the transformative technology, and has since dedicated her life to being the best coach possible for her clients. She has personally helped train more than one thousand life coaches worldwide for The Coaches Training Institute and OneTaste.

Nicole Daedone, Founder of OneTaste, recognizes Mai for her "Heart of Service." Her clients simply call her "AMAIZING!"

ADDENDUM

What Do I Do Now?

I hope you enjoyed reading this book. More importantly, I hope you use what you've learned to attract the love and life you want by tending to your *peasant* and integrating your *princess* and *priestess* into your life.

In my experience, learning about the 3Ps™ initially creates a tremendous relief in your tired and overwhelmed *peasant* body. But reading alone does not create lasting change, and most definitely won't bring you the relationship and success you want. Why? Because the *peasant* is a tough one. She stubbornly resists letting love in. She thinks she has learned enough, and will try to figure this out on her own. As good as the *princess* and *priestess's* help sounds to her, she does not trust them. She will pretend to be them, speak for them in your head as if she were them, but you will soon find out that she is back to her old tricks—doing everything by herself, feeling resentful that she is being called out as a *peasant*, and, consequently, is not being appreciated again. It is an endless loop of self-destruction.

If you read this book and are moved by this concept, I urge you to take action right away before your *peasant* forgets and gets all wound up with life's demands. I would like to invite you and a friend to attend my next HotLifeHotLove™ 2 Day Live Event. This is an awesome event where you'll be with like-minded women who want the same shift in their lives that you do. You will be loved, adored, and cherished by me, my Hot Love team, and my graduate clients. My clients love this work so much that they come back year after year. They even travel with me to Sweden, where I also offer my work, to support women like you.

See the following pages for more details about this invitation. Thank you for being the hard-working mom whom you are, raising kids, building businesses, leading task forces, loving your community, and doing big things in your most humble ways. I am delighted to support you.

I wish you the hottest love, the most thriving business, and the greatest life. HotLifeHotLove™ Baby!!!

Love, Love, Love,

Mai Vu

SPECIAL INVITATION

Attend the HotLifeHotLove™ 2 Day Live Event on FULL SCHOLARSHIP

I would like to invite you and a friend to attend my live event so that I can help your *peasant* heal and your *princess* and *priestess* blossom. I am offering a FULL SCHOLARSHIP for you two to attend the event. That's a total value of $1,994 - for free!

To commit you to take action and come, I am requesting a seat deposit of $97. It will be refunded when you get your name badge. I know how *peasants* operate. You read this book, get inspired, see this invitation, and say, "YES! I will come." Immediately, or two days later, you forget why you said yes. Your *peasant* starts to make up a story that says you don't need this. Then you numbly go back to the same ol' grind. But this time you have a new tool to beat yourself up with, by saying to yourself, "Oh, don't be such a *peasant*!" That's what people do. They learn a new thing, then they use it against themselves.

When you come to the 2 Day Event, you will be immersed in love. The HotLifeHotLove™ 2 Day Event is designed to show you what being loved, adored, and cherished really look like, through the concepts, the experience, the community, and the conversations. You will discover how to:

- Tend to your *peasant*

- Gently identify the many ways you resist love

- Be introduced to your *princess* self

- Learn to let love in

- Understand men and how they work with your 3Ps™

- Listen to your *priestess* guidance

- Practice the language of the Princess and the Priestess
- Make more money
- Command more respect
- Be more supported
- Have a much greater impact on the world

Hundreds of people from the US, Canada, and Sweden/Norway/Denmark have attended the HotLifeHotLove™ 2 Day Live Event. The feedback is consistent:

"Powerful, Essential. Life-changing. Inspiring"

and "Mai (May), is aMAIzing!!!"

Join us. Say YES to letting love in.

What People are saying about the HotLifeHotLoveTM 2 Day Event and Mai Vu:

"This is my fourth HotLifeHotLove™ Event, I learn something new each time. I always walk away filled with love and inspiration for what's possible in my life." ~ Kelly Wolf

"It was Mai who got me where I am today—truly nurtured, pampered, and feeling deeply at peace and in flow with my life. I am honored and excited to recommend Mai's book to you." ~ Cindy Ashton

"Mai, I will always be grateful to you for helping me release parts of myself that were no longer serving me." ~ Cindy Roemer

"Why do I keep coming to assist at the HotLifeHotLove™ Event? Because it feeds my soul. And I love the women who come." ~ Jo Ellen Neihart

"I have a lot of fun living out my hot hot hot! life ;) Thank you!" ~ Anna Åberg

"Mai, I am so grateful for you and your work. You helped me launch my business and my love life. Your program surpassed my expectations. Thank YOU!" ~ Denise B.

"Mai is the real deal! Her 3Ps™ concept will change your life. It has changed mine." ~ Darla Crecerelle

"Mai, I am so grateful for you and your work. You helped me launch my business and my love life. Your program surpassed my expectations. Thank YOU!" ~ Denise B.

"I have learned so much from Mai and I can say my life is better. My relationship with my husband is better, my relationship with other family members is better. But most importantly my relationship with me is so much better." ~Karen Sabetan

"No other coach has ever been a true partner in my journey like Mai Vu has. I don't know how she does it— but she is amazing at it!!!" ~ Andrea Williams

Join My Community:

http://www.hotlifehotlove.com/divorced-moms-dating-guide

Here you can connect with other women who have learned the 3Ps™ and who have gotten support from the community. You can also learn about upcoming events and programs.

Download a set of printable worksheets

http://maivucoach.com/book-worksheets/

HOTLIFEHOTLOVE™ 2DAY LIVE EVENT CERTIFICATE

Mai Vu and her **HotLifeHotLove™ Team** invite you and a friend to attend the **HotLifeHotLove™-2Day Event** as our guests*. For more information and to register, please visit: http://www.hotlifehotlove.com/

For more information, visit the website www.HotLifeHotLove.com or contact Mai@HotLifeHotLove.com   www.MaiVuCoach.com

Made in the USA
Middletown, DE
06 July 2017